Dinghy Sailing

Dinghy Sailing

Sarah Ell

NEW HOLLAND

First published in 2001, this edition published in 2009 by
New Holland Publishers Ltd
London • Cape Town • Sydney • Auckland

86 Edgware Road
London W2 2EA
United Kingdom

80 McKenzie Street
Cape Town 8001
South Africa

Unit 1, 66 Gibbes Street
Chatswood, NSW 2067
Australia

218 Lake Road
Northcote, Auckland
New Zealand

ISBN 9 781 84773 413 6

Publisher: Mariëlle Renssen
Managing Editors: Claudia Dos Santos, Mari Roberts
Managing Art Editor: Peter Bosman
Editor: Sean Fraser
Designer and illustrator: Ben Latham
Production: Myrna Collins

Consultant: Robin Sjoberg (UK)

Reproduction by Hirt & Carter (Cape) Pty Ltd
Printed and bound by
Craft Print International Ltd, Singapore

6 8 10 9 7 5

Disclaimer

Author's acknowledgements

My sincere thanks to Mathew Brown, for assisting with the text, his advice, support and modelling, and helping to organize the photographic shoot; Murrays Bay Sailing Club; Takapuna Sailing Centre; Andrea Brabant; Rhys Johnston; my family for their continued support and encouragement.

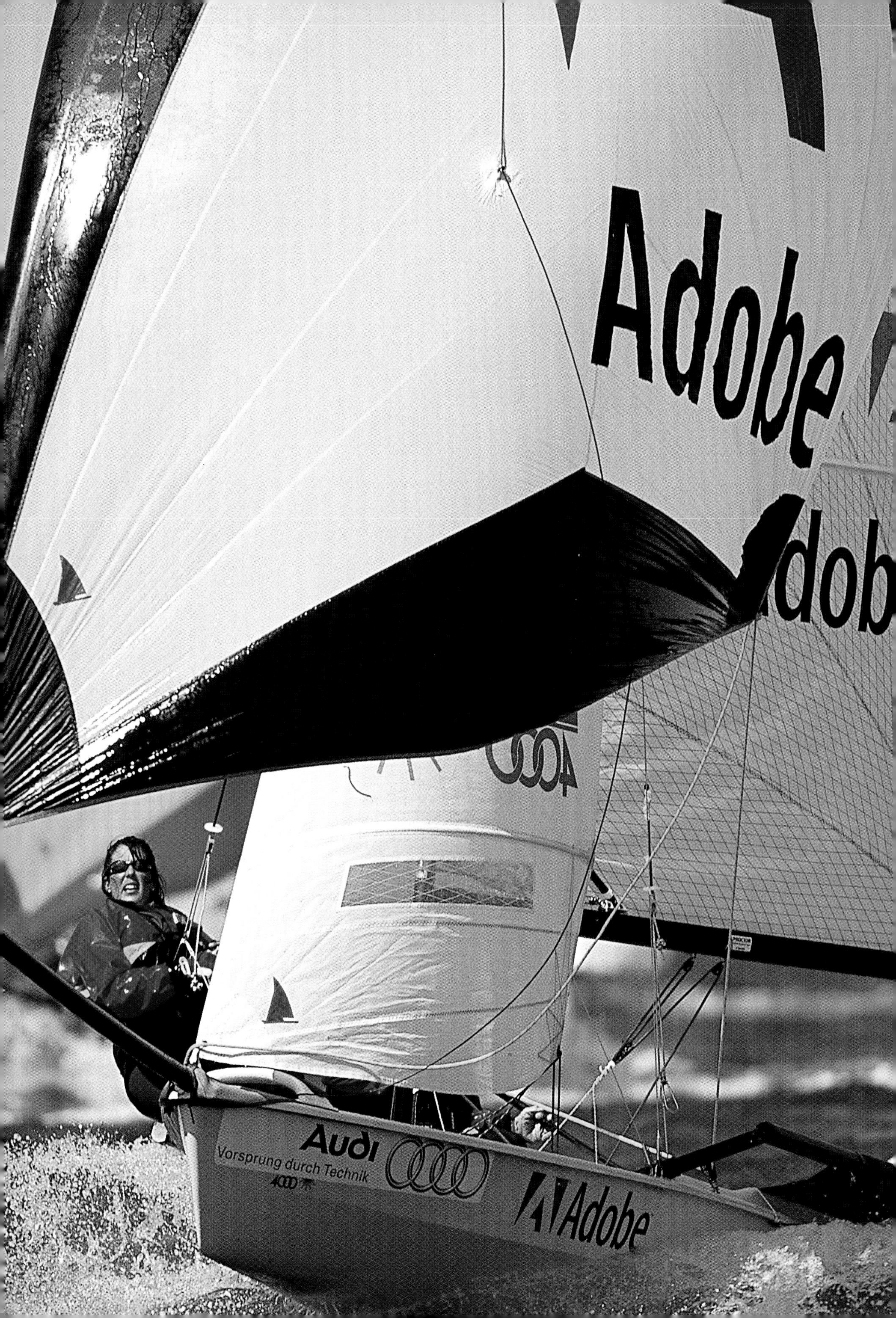
Adobe
Audi
Vorsprung durch Technik
Adobe

Contents

Welcome to Dinghy Sailing

there is a certain mystique to sailing. The word itself conjures up glamorous images of large, sail-powered ships such as the clippers that once ran the world's trade routes, the super yachts of the extremely wealthy that ply the Mediterranean and Caribbean, and the Grand Prix racers of the America's Cup and the Volvo Ocean Race (formerly the Whitbread). Many people think of sailing as an elite sport, a rich man's game enjoyed only by professionals with years of experience, or those with enough money to pay someone to sail the boat while they lie around on the deck drinking champagne. In fact, there is a popular saying that being involved in sailing is like standing in a cold shower tearing up wads of cash; another defines a yacht as a hole in the water into which you pour money.

A sport for all

Sailing is accessible to almost anyone. You do not have to be rich. At the very basic level, you don't even have to own a boat to sail. Nor do you have to be particularly fit, or even a talented sportsperson. Men and women, young and old, can enjoy everything sailing has to offer — be it the thrill of speed, the intellectual and technical challenge, the extension to your social life, simple recreation, intense competition, or just a way to while away a sunny afternoon.

Dinghy sailing, like keelboat sailing, is often considered by 'landlubbers' — non-sailors — to be highly technical, a minefield of complex jargon and inexplicable manoeuvres, about as exciting for spectators as watching grass grow. Sailing revolves around a force that cannot be seen by the naked eye — the wind — and uses the laws of physics to enable a boat to move across the surface of another unpredictable medium — water. However, at its most basic level, sailing is a simple pleasure — more of an art than a science, which has more to do with instinct and feeling than knowing all the technical tricks in the book. Dinghy sailing can be enjoyed immediately as an observer or as an active participant, with even greater pleasure and satisfaction coming with confidence and experience.

One of the critical elements of all physical adventure sports such as sailing is the issue of safety. Always wear a well-fitting buoyancy aid, and familiarize yourself with the 'rules of the road' and safety procedures. See also pages 82—83 and Health hazards on page 85.

DINGHY SAILING IS BOTH A FUN AND A CHALLENGING SPORT THAT CAN BE ENJOYED BY PEOPLE OF ALL AGES.

opposite WHETHER YOU SAIL ALONE OR WITH FRIENDS, THE BASIC SKILLS OF DINGHY SAILING ARE EASY TO MASTER.

Enjoying the spectacle

Major yacht-racing events have brought sailing into living rooms around the world, giving the sport a much higher profile, but at the same time making it look complex and technical. However, it is worth remembering that, while watching these professional sailors do their work, each and every one of them started as a novice. Almost without exception, every one of those highly skilled — and highly paid — men and women started to learn to sail in a dinghy, and many are still active dinghy sailors.

All the participants who sail at the Olympic Games, the pinnacle of competitive sailing, started out by learning the parts of a boat, getting the feel of how to sail, and working out how to steer the boat in the direction they wanted to sail. And they still get the same kick out of arriving at the beach on a sunny day, pushing off into the water, feeling the wind on their face and the water part before them as the boat powers up and sails away. It's a feeling you can't buy and, to a certain extent, can't describe — which is why you have to give it a try.

Where did it all begin?

For thousands of years, sailing was not a sport, but a practical means of transport. From the *feluccas* of the Middle East and Mediterranean through the coastal sailing vessels and raiding boats of the Vikings to the grand clippers that plied the world's trade routes, ships using sail power were the primary means of transport. Smaller sail-powered boats have been used throughout the centuries for local voyages and fishing trips, and some of the earliest racing dinghies descended from these working boats. For many years, fishermen, whalers and other seamen participated in regattas in their working boats. In New Zealand, for example, the establishment of the nation's then-capital at Auckland in 1842 was celebrated by a series of boat races, including a race between sailing whaleboats. Throughout the early years of this annual event, now said to be the world's largest one-day regatta, all competitors took part in working boats: coastal traders and sail-powered fishing vessels. Similar events of various scales were held all over the world, wherever there were working sailboats.

WITH NEW DINGHY CLASSES AND HIGH-TECH SAILS AND EQUIPMENT, SAILING IS BECOMING INCREASINGLY EXCITING AS A SPECTATOR SPORT.

WITH THE INCREASING POPULARITY OF SAILING, MORE AND MORE SPECTATORS ARE ATTENDING TOP EVENTS WORDWIDE.

THE LASER, DESIGNED BY CANADIAN BRUCE KIRBY, IS ONE OF THE MOST POPULAR DINGHY CLASSES IN THE WORLD TODAY.

The origins of racing

From the mid-19th century, racing large yachts slowly became a recreational pursuit for the wealthy. The America's Cup, first sailed in 1852, brought the sport to the popular attention of the upper classes, and is now one of the longest-standing sporting competitions in the world. Although it featured as a sport at the Olympic Games from 1896, sailing only really started to take off as a recreational pursuit for less-moneyed participants in the mid-20th century. Larger yachts became cheaper and easier to build, and new materials — such as plywood and epoxy glues — caught the imagination of innovative small-boat designers such as Jack Holt in the UK and John Spencer in New Zealand. This saw the creation of new types of dinghies, which were lightweight and could be built without too much difficulty by amateurs, rather than the time-consuming techniques that were used on clinker-built vessels, which had previously restricted boatbuilding to highly skilled tradesmen.

The introduction of fibreglass construction techniques in the 1960s and 1970s also enabled manufacturers to start mass-producing identical boats at greatly reduced cost. The new methods created lightweight, easy-to-maintain boats that required no time-consuming sanding, painting and varnishing, and were robust enough to take the odd knock. They could be towed easily, or even transported on the roof of a car. They also had simple rigging systems, with just one or two sails, and were easy to set up and sail. Most of all, these boats were primarily designed for fun — whether in a racing situation or just cruising.

One of the most popular of the new dinghy classes was the Laser, designed in the early 1970s by Canadian Bruce Kirby. The Laser has since grown to be the largest single-handed dinghy class in the world, with more than 170,000 boats across the globe. It is a testament to its combination of simplicity and performance that it was named as an Olympic dinghy class, making its debut in 1996.

Having a go

You may already have some experience of sailing. You may have gone out for a day on a keelboat, or for a spin on a catamaran with a friend. You might know people who are active sailors — but have never understood a word they are talking about. You may have gone sailing as a child, or on holiday, but never had the opportunity to follow it up. Alternatively, your only contact with sailing might be through what you have seen on television or read in the papers. It doesn't matter. You don't have to have come from a sailing family or be experienced in watersports. Almost anyone can try sailing.

One of the best opportunities to try sailing is while on holiday. Many sea- and lakeside holiday resorts have their own fleet of boats, with professional instructors standing by to teach you the basics. The boats at these resorts are likely to be of a simple, easy-to-handle type — beach catamarans such as the Hobie Cat or a trainer dinghy such as the Topper. Going out for a sail with someone who knows what they are doing, giving you time and space to see if you like the feel of it, is a good way to find out if sailing is right for you. This is an especially good option if you live far from the water, and do not want to invest time and money only to find out later that dinghy sailing is not suitable for you.

Another option is to enquire at your local sailing club whether one of their members would be prepared to take you out for a sail to 'test the waters'. Quite often, experienced dinghy sailors will be looking for crew for a double-handed boat, and will be only too pleased to take someone out for a sail who might become a convert to the sport. Many sailing clubs also run specific learn-to-sail programmes for adults as well as children.

As with any organized sport, sailing clubs are always keen to attract new members, and many offer courses at very reasonable rates, using boats belonging to the club. Local schools and marine education centres may also run theoretical and practical courses for beginners keen to become involved in the adventure of dinghy sailing.

For more information, contact your local council or sporting body for the name and details of your local club, or consult the list of sailing associations listed on pages 92–93. These organizations and institutions may help to put you in touch with a local club or community sailing-school programme that offers introductory courses.

MANY OF THE WORLD'S TOP PROFESSIONAL SAILORS LEARNT THEIR SKILLS AS CHILDREN, BUT IT'S NEVER TOO LATE TO LEARN.

Obviously, there are some risks involved in sailing, but a combination of adequate training, sufficient safety equipment, sound knowledge and experience on the water will give you the confidence to handle virtually any situation. Always wear a buoyancy aid suited to your size and build; this will provide adequate support and a reliable 'safety net', while not restricting your movement on the water. See also Safety at sea on page 78, Safety equipment on page 79, and Health hazards on page 85.

Some people feel anxious about sailing because it involves too many factors that appear to be beyond their immediate control – the fluctuations of the wind and waves, for example – but experienced sailors know that although they cannot dictate how these elements behave, they can learn to read them, understand them, exploit them and adjust the yacht to respond to them.

It would be unwise to attempt to learn to sail without some confidence on the water, an ability to swim and a well-fitting buoyancy aid. Chances are, you will fall overboard sooner or later, and even if it doesn't happen immediately, your fear that it might happen at any moment could spoil your enjoyment of sailing.

Some countries have boat-licensing systems, under which the individuals in control of boats on the water must have certain basic qualifications. Even if you wish to do nothing more than spend some recreational time on the water, it is wise to master the basics of boat safety. Most sailing and coastguard organizations offer a range of courses, which usually include a beginner's class that covers the basics: rules of the road at sea, safety and emergency procedures, buoys, beacons and light systems, basic boat handling, knots, first aid and the weather. Even if you only plan to go out for a quick sail in very fine weather, unexpected difficulties can develop very quickly when you are out on the water.

Armed with the right safety equipment, knowledge and experience, dinghy sailing can be a thoroughly enjoyable adventure. As Scottish writer Kenneth Grahame wrote in *The Wind in the Willows*, 'There is nothing – absolutely nothing – half so much worth doing as simply messing about in boats'.

LIKE ALL PHYSICAL ACTIVITIES – AND MOST ESPECIALLY WATERSPORTS – DINGHY SAILING ENTAILS SOME ELEMENT OF RISK. BUOYANCY AIDS, SUCH AS LIFE JACKETS, ARE THUS ESSENTIAL SAFETY EQUIPMENT WHENEVER YOU ARE ON THE WATER.

Understanding the Basics

One of the features that can make sailing seem quite incomprehensible to the uninitiated is the unique language sailors seem to speak. A boat doesn't just have a front and a back, or a pointy end and a flat end, it has a bow and a stern; left and right are port and starboard; the ropes are called halyards and sheets. When it comes to manoeuvring, the jargon becomes even more complex. There's tacking and gybing, bearing away, coming up and bearing away... And many elements have more than one name! You might wonder if you will ever master the language.

The good news is that these terms are easy to learn. Don't worry if you can't remember them all right away — you will be jabbering away like an old salt in no time!

Getting to know your boat

The solid part of the sailing dinghy — the part that rests in the water — is called the hull. The part of the hull above the water is called the topsides, while its bottom is simply called the bottom! The top edges of the boat, at the upper end of the topsides, are called gunwales (pronounced *gunnels*), and the flat area that covers the upper surface of the boat is called the deck. Set into this is usually a cockpit, where the crew sit and from where they sail the boat. Some boats, such as the Laser dinghy, are mostly deck and very little cockpit, while many older designs have no deck at all and are open right through to the bow or have a small deck area forward of the mast. The flat, vertical area at the stern, to which the rudder is attached, is called the transom.

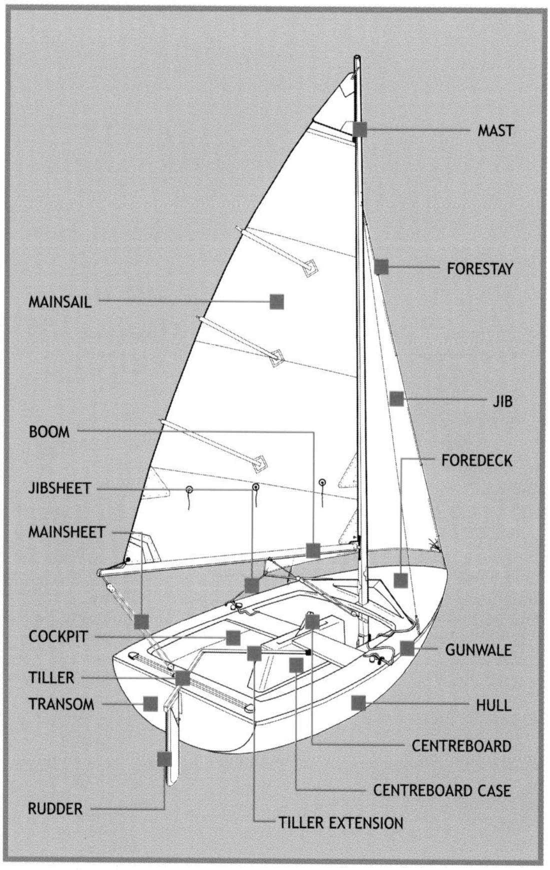

Diagram labels

MAST
FORESTAY
MAINSAIL
JIB
BOOM
FOREDECK
JIBSHEET
MAINSHEET
COCKPIT
GUNWALE
TILLER
TRANSOM
HULL
CENTREBOARD
CENTREBOARD CASE
RUDDER
TILLER EXTENSION

Following the wind

Windward This is the side over which wind is blowing. If you are sailing with wind blowing over the port side of the boat, port is the windward side. This is also known as the weather side, and objects on this side are 'to weather', because that is the side from which the weather — in other words, the wind — is coming.

Leeward The opposite side to the windward side of the boat is the leeward (pronounced *loo-ard*) side, because it is in the lee, or shelter, of the sails. Objects and other boats are referred to as being 'to leeward'.

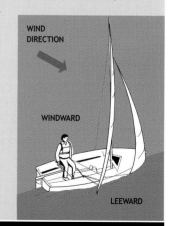

WIND DIRECTION
WINDWARD
LEEWARD

opposite ONCE A SAILOR HAS MASTERED ALL THE BASICS, DINGHY RACING PROVIDES A CHALLENGING OPTION.

Rigging

The equipment attached to the hull and decks is known as the boat's rigging. The mast and boom are known as spars and the wires that hold them in place are called stays, or standing rigging. All the ropes are known as running rigging. These usually run through and are controlled by a number of small fixtures such as pulleys, called blocks, and secured by cleats. The blocks vary in size and may include ratchet mechanisms, which make the wheel inside the pulley run only one way, to help you control the ropes. The cleats are used to fix ropes into position when they do not need to be adjusted.

The mast — the vertical wooden, metal or composite pole that sticks up from the middle of the boat — and the horizontal boom attached to it are known collectively as spars. These are a considerable refinement on the complicated systems of the past, where square-rigged ships had several masts with yardarms running horizontally across them, to hold their square sails at an angle to the breeze.

The boom attaches to the mast at the gooseneck, a flexible fitting that allows the boom to swing through an angle of up to 180°, from side to side.

On more basic, modern dinghies such as the Laser, the mast is often freestanding, inserted into a hole in the deck and secured with elastic bungee cord. However, many boats, especially the larger ones, have wires that hold the mast upright and in the correct position. These wire ropes, known as stays, usually lead down to the bow (the forestay) and to the sides of the boat, parallel with the mast (sidestays or shrouds). Sometimes, there is also a stay, or stays, leading to the boat's stern (backstays).

Point of sail

The point of sail is the angle to the wind at which a boat is sailing. The two main points of sail are upwind and downwind, but within downwind there is reaching, which is sailing at an angle between 50—170° to the wind direction, and running or sailing flat-off, which is sailing at an angle of nearly 180° to the wind direction.

There are also different types of reaching: tight or close reaching and beam reaching and broad reaching.

Sailing slightly off the wind with the sails of the boat slightly eased is called tight reaching or close reaching. When the wind is coming across the boat at a 90° angle, this is called a beam reach. If you are sailing at an even greater angle to the wind direction — between 100° and 170°, for example — you are then sailing on a broad reach.

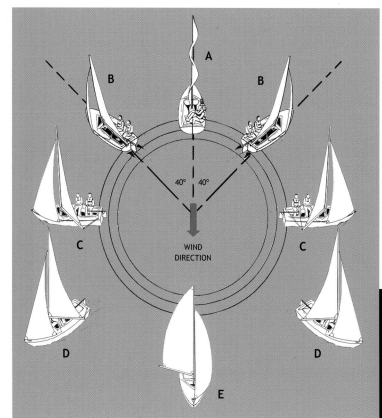

POINTS OF SAIL

A HEAD-TO-WIND

B SAILING ON THE WIND

C A BEAM REACH

D A BROAD REACH

E SAILING FLAT-OFF

As in any sport, there are fundamental terms you should know before starting out. If you have had some exposure to boats and the water, you may already be familiar with some of these terms, but because they are so integral to sailing, you will need to understand precisely what these mean if you are to sail with confidence.

Port This is the nautical term for left. The port side of the boat is the left-hand side when you are facing forward. It is represented by the colour red in the international lights and buoyage system. The word is also used along with åother sailing terms, such as 'port tack' (sailing along on an angle so that the wind is coming over the port side of the boat) and 'leaving a mark to port' (sailing around a buoy or mark so that the port side of the boat is closest to it). One way to remember the definition of the word is to memorize the phrase: 'Is there any red *port* wine *left*?' Other people remember that port is a shorter word than starboard, and left is a shorter word than right!

Starboard This is the term for right, and is used in the same ways as 'port'. In the international system, starboard is indicated as green.

Bow This is the front end of the boat or, less academically, 'the pointy bit'. It is also called the stem as used in the nautical expression 'from stem to stern'.

Stern The stern is the back end of the boat. The term 'astern' indicates something behind the boat, such as 'the other yacht is passing astern'.

Beam The widest part of the boat, usually roughly in the centre, is called the beam. This term is used to indicate a relationship with the middle of the boat, for example 'we are abeam of that other boat' or 'the wind is now forward of the beam'.

Forward Pronounced *for'ard*, forward is towards the front of the boat or the bow, and is used in such phrases as 'forward of the beam' and 'move your weight forward'.

Aft Towards the back or stern (see above) of the boat.

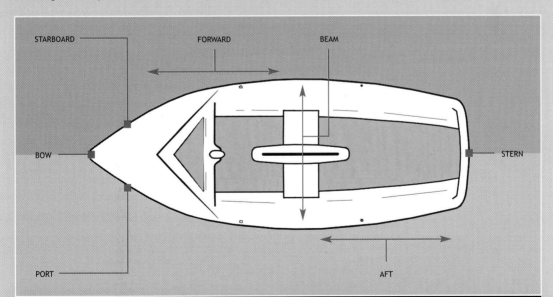

STARBOARD FORWARD BEAM

BOW STERN

PORT AFT

KNOWING THE CORRECT TERMS FOR THE INDIVIDUAL PARTS OF THE DINGHY, AND INDEED ANY SAILING VESSEL, WILL MAKE IT EASIER TO UNDERSTAND WHAT OTHER SAILORS ARE SAYING, AND WILL HELP YOU GIVE AND RECEIVE CLEAR INSTRUCTIONS WHEN SAILING WITH A CREW, ALLOWING FOR SAFE AND ENJOYABLE SAILING.

Sails

The boat's sails are attached to the spars. In the case of a single-handed dinghy such as the Laser, there is usually only one sail, the mainsail. The vertical edge of this large, triangular sail is attached to the mast, and its bottom edge to the boom.

On two-handed dinghies, there is often a jib, head-sail or foresail as well. (On larger boats, when this sail is large enough to overlap the mainsail at its back corner, it is called a genoa jib, often reffered to as a genny.) This is flown in front of the mast, with its long, angled edge attached to the forestay, and its vertical edge and bottom free-flying.

Many larger dinghies also carry an extra downwind sail, called a spinnaker or gennaker. The spinnaker has a symmetrical, curved shape and is flown off its own

THE 470 HAS A MORE COMPLEX SAIL PLAN THAN THE SINGLE-HANDED LASER, AND IS CREWED BY TWO SAILORS.

THE MAST IS INSERTED INTO THE SLEEVE ON THE VERTICAL EDGE OF THE LASER'S MAINSAIL, WHILE THE BOTTOM CORNERS OF THE SAIL ARE ATTACHED TO THE BOOM.

boom, forward of the mast. A gennaker — a cross between a genoa and a spinnaker — is a new type of downwind sail that is asymmetrical, and is usually flown with one corner fixed to a bowsprit sticking out of the front of the boat. See also page 20.

These sails are hauled up into position and held there by halyards, which run up inside the mast, and are controlled by sheets. The mainsheet runs from the boom, through a series of blocks or pulleys, down to an attachment on the cockpit floor. (Some boats have aft-mainsheet systems, in which the mainsheet runs down to a bridle or traveller running across the back of the boat.)

The pair of jib sheets attach to the free-flying corner of the jib and run back through a system of blocks to each side of the cockpit. These make the ropes easier to hold and control. Only the leeward sheet of the pair is used to control the shape of the sail at any time.

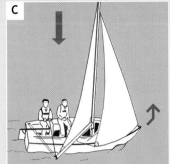

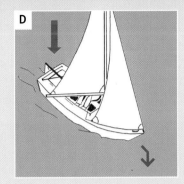

A Upwind Sailing upwind is sailing as close to the wind direction as possible. Yachts cannot sail directly into the wind, and can only sail at a course of about 35–40° to its direction. This is also known as sailing hard-on or on the wind, sailing close-hauled, sailing to windward or beating. Upwind is also used to refer to objects, destinations and so on that are 'to windward'.

B Downwind Sailing downwind means sailing in any direction with the wind coming from behind the boat. This is also known as sailing off the wind, and can be as little as just 5° or 10° away from hard-on, right through to where the wind is coming from directly astern (when the

boat's stern is at 90° to the wind). Objects or destinations can be 'downwind' of your current position if your boat is positioned between them and the direction from which the wind is blowing.

C Luffing up Luffing up, or 'coming up', is steering the boat's bow up into or towards the wind. This action is used to bring the boat onto an upwind course, or beyond it. A full luff involves steering the boat so that its bow faces into the wind, and the sails are flapping. Be warned, however, that 'coming up' does not mean that the tiller 'comes up' towards you; in fact, you push the tiller away to come up. So, when you steer 'up', the tiller moves down!

D Bearing away Bearing away, or 'coming down', is the action of steering the boat's bow away from the wind direction. This is done by pulling the tiller towards you — it moves up so that you can go down.

E Tacking This means changing direction when sailing upwind, so the bow passes through the eye of the wind, which then blows across the other side of the boat. Making several direction changes is known as beating, or tacking into the wind.

F Gybing Gybing means changing direction when sailing downwind, so that the stern passes through the eye of the wind, which then blows across the other side of the boat.

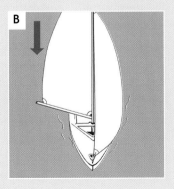

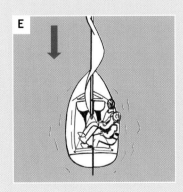

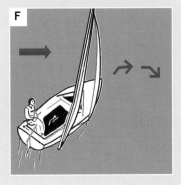

Parts of a sail

Each of the edges and each corner of a sail has a name. The bottom of the sail is the foot, the leading edge is the luff, and the trailing edge is the leach; the curved portion, outside the line from the boom end to the masthead, is called the roach. The top corner, to which the halyard is attached, is called the head. The forward corner of the triangle — the right angle on the mainsail, and the forward corner of the triangle on the jib — is called the tack, and the aft corner, onto which the sheets are attached on the jib, is called the clew. Because spinnakers are symmetrical, they have a head and two clews, one on each lower corner. An asymmetrical gennaker is more like a jib: it has a head, a tack fixed to the bowsprit, and a clew, onto which the sheets are attached.

As well as the mainsheet, there are usually three other controls attached to the mainsail. The outhaul runs between the clew of the sail and the aft end of the boom, and is used to adjust the foot of the sail, making it loose or tight along the boom. The cunningham runs from the tack of the sail down to a control on the deck or in the cockpit, and is used to adjust the tension of the luff of the sail. The boom vang, or kicking strap, runs on an angle from the underside of the boom down to the lower part of the mast. This block-and-tackle system is used to keep the boom down and under control.

Sheets and other running rigging were used to be made of natural fibres. Now there is a range of high-tech cordage for sailing boats. Today most ropes are made of nylon and other synthetic fibres. Materials such as Kevlar and Spectra are light and strong, but may stretch and tend to deteriorate in strong sunlight. Polypropylene and polythene ropes will float, which makes them useful for tow ropes, although they are not as strong as nylon and polyester. Polyester and polypropylene ropes are most commonly used for sheets and halyards on small boats.

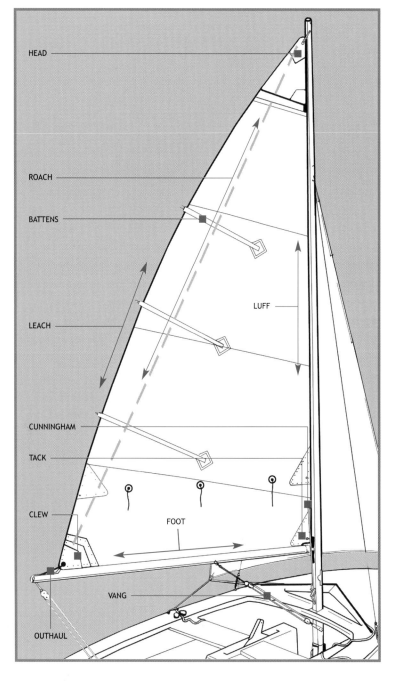

HEAD
ROACH
BATTENS
LUFF
LEACH
CUNNINGHAM
TACK
CLEW
FOOT
VANG
OUTHAUL

ON A REACH, THE CENTREBOARD IS PARTIALLY LIFTED TO REDUCE DRAG WHILE CONTINUING TO PREVENT SIDE-SLIP.

THE DAGGERBOARD, AS OPPOSED TO THE SWINGING CENTREBOARD, IS THE SIMPLEST FORM OF FOIL.

Foils

All boats have underwater appendages that help keep them balanced and moving efficiently forward through the water. These are carefully shaped to reduce drag underwater and help the boat sail to windward.

Larger sailing boats have a lead keel, which helps stop the boat tipping over. All sailing dinghies have a centreboard or daggerboard, which slots through the centre of the hull just aft of the mast. This stops the boat from being pushed sideways when sailing upwind.

The rudder is attached to the stern and is used to steer. It is controlled by the tiller, which may also have a tiller extension or toe stick, which makes it more comfortable to steer when sitting on the side decks. The rudder may be attached to fittings (gudgeons) on the transom by sliding a metal pin (pintle) through the holes in them. This allows the rudder blade to pivot according to the actions of the tiller.

Other equipment

The skipper and crew slip their feet and ankles under the hiking straps on the cockpit floor when leaning out, or hiking (see also page 30), to keep the boat flat.

A useful piece of equipment is a mast-mounted wind indicator. This can be as simple as a little flag (burgee), or a more sophisticated plastic vane, to show the direction from which the wind is blowing in relation to the boat. This is mounted on the top of the mast, and is invaluable when you are learning to feel the wind.

All tied up

Practise these simple knots until you can do them without the aid of diagrams.

A Bowline This is used to form a bight, or loop, at the end of a line — such as when attaching a sheet to the clew of a sail, or tying a boat to a wharf.

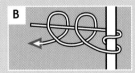

B Round turn and two half hitches These are used to secure a rope to a spar or ring.

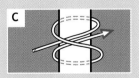

C Clove hitch The clove hitch is most commonly used to fasten a line to a spar or post.

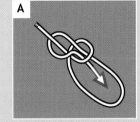

D Figure of eight This is used as a stopper knot at the end of a rope so that it cannot run back through a cleat or block.

Getting

Equipped

Sometimes, it might seem that there are as many types of sailing dinghy as there are sailors. New methods of construction and innovative designs have resulted in a proliferation of dinghy classes with a wide range of sizes.

A class of its own

Some classes are local inventions, found only in a specific area, while others are official international classes, recognized by the International Sailing Federation (ISAF) and governed by design and sail-plan rules. Most of these are racing classes, for which national and world championships are held. While some classes are governed by rules covering length, sail area, weight and so on, modern mass-production techniques mean that some are now entirely one-design. This means the boats are all precisely the same, with identical-shaped hulls popped out of a mould or built over a plug. These boats are fitted with the same gear and fittings, and carry the same sails, so they are raced on an equal footing. This makes for very close, exciting racing that places the emphasis on the ability of individual sailors.

At the other end of the scale are the development classes, which tend to attract amateur designers and engineers. These classes have loose or flexible design rules and encourage innovation. The America's Cup Class is a rather outsized example of this.

The construction

There have been many important advances in boat-building technology in the past 30 or 40 years. Most modern sailing dinghies are now made of (F)GRP — (fibre)glass-reinforced plastic — which makes them easy to produce, hard-wearing, buoyant and light-weight. GRP boats usually have rounded underwater shapes, which makes them round-bilge yachts. These designs are usually simple to set up and responsive on the water. However, 'responsive' can also mean 'unforgiving', and you may fall out a few times!

Many boats are also still made from plywood which, as well as being lightweight, has the advantage of being workable by amateur builders. Many yachts built of this material have hard chine hulls, which have straight faces with angled joins between them.

above MANY MODERN CLASSES ARE ONE-DESIGN, PRODUCED FROM AN IDENTICAL MOULD OR PLUG.

opposite TODAY'S DINGHIES ARE LIGHTWEIGHT AND EASY TO MANOEUVRE ON LAND AND ON SEA.

The materials

There are still timber sailing dinghies with clinker-built hulls, but they are heavier and less responsive than modern designs. If this is not a priority, you may be able to buy an old classic and learn to sail in style.

As well as the hull material, the type of material used for the spars also varies. Older boats usually have wooden masts and booms, whereas modern ones are made of aluminium or other metals. High-tech boats will have spars of composite materials such as carbon fibre, which is very light and strong, yet flexible. In some classes, materials for masts and other spars are controlled by class rules. Sail materials may also vary from white terylene sailcloth to shiny golden Kevlar or even high-tech, see-through Mylar.

One hand or two?

Most dinghies are classified either single- or double-handed, although some single-handers can take a second crew person. By and large, a single-handed dinghy will have a mainsail only, while double-handers will have a jib and, in many cases, a spinnaker.

What type of boat do I want?

If you are learning to sail with a friend, or through a school, you may have little choice. However, if you do have a choice of class, talk to your local sailing club and other sailors. You may be better off buying or borrowing the class of boat other people in your area own or sail, so they can assist you — and provide someone to check your performance against when you race.

The trapeze

Some performance-oriented double-handed boats have a trapeze system for the crew, and sometimes the skipper. This system enables the crew to extend their weight further outboard. This extra leverage means that these boats can carry larger sails. The crew wears a harness that clips onto a line which runs down from the mast, and stand on the gunwale rather than just hiking out. Trapezing takes some practice as you learn to maintain your balance, but is an enormous amount of fun.

TRAPEZE SYSTEMS ENABLE DINGHIES TO CARRY LARGER, MORE POWERFUL SAILS AND OFFER A FAST AND EXCITING RIDE.

Do I want to sail with other people?

This will determine whether you choose a single- or double-handed dinghy. Sailing a single-hander puts all the emphasis on your own skills and decisions, while in a double-handed dinghy you share the load. One of the best ways to start learning is to crew for an experienced sailor on a double-hander, trimming the jib and perhaps the spinnaker while learning the basic principles and getting the feel. It is perhaps easier to learn to steer a single-handed boat, because only your weight, positioning and trimming will make a difference to how the boat performs. When you carry out an action, you will be able to feel how the boat responds. On a double-handed boat, the actions and movements of the crew will affect how the boat sails.

What size do I need?

Think about your own size, age and strength, and that of your crew. Not only do you want a boat you are able to handle on land, launching and retrieving, but also one you can sail without being overpowered. Most classes have an 'ideal weight' range based on the sail area. For example, you need to be at least 75kg (165 lb) to sail a full-rig Laser, or you will not be able to exert enough power to balance the force of the wind. Also, the smaller and lighter the boat is, the more responsive it will be.

Where will I be sailing?

You need to consider the wind and wave conditions typical of your area. There is little point in buying a lightweight, fast, planing boat if you are always sailing in choppy, swell conditions. Likewise, you won't have as much fun sailing a heavy old tub if you will be sailing in light winds and flat water.

How safe is the dinghy?

You will need to look at buoyancy and how the cockpit is drained — and whether the dinghy will be easy to right when capsized (because this will happen!). Look for a boat with generous built-in flotation and a self-draining cockpit.

How easy is it to set up?

When starting out, you need a dinghy that is quickly and easily rigged. Racing boats can be quite technical, and need fine-tuning. For the beginner, you want a vessel on which you can simply hoist the sails and get out on the water.

Why do I want it?

Consider the long term. Do you want to race? Will you be happy just cruising around, enjoying the sea? If you think you would like to race, look for a class that is raced in your area. Check with local sailors and find a class that is not too technical for beginners, but which offers performance and racing potential.

Where will I keep it?

Do you have a car suitable for a trailer or car-topping a boat? Will you need to keep it at a local yacht club, trailer park or dinghy lockers? Buy a boat that is easy to handle and will allow you to store it near your home or sailing waters.

WHERE YOU PLAN TO STORE AND LAUNCH YOUR DINGHY IS AN IMPORTANT CONSIDERATION WHEN CHOOSING A CLASS TO SAIL.

Single-handed classes

There are a number of single-handed classes of dinghy.

Byte

The Byte was designed in the 1990s by Ian Bruce, one of the developers of the Laser. Its popularity means it now has its own world championship. It was designed to be sailed by sailors of 45–65kg (100–145 lb), making it suitable for female sailors and teenage boys. The Byte is 3.65m (12ft) long and weighs about 45kg (100 lb), so it is easy to launch. For more information, visit the website www.byteclass.org

International Topper

The Topper is made of lightweight, injection-moulded polypropylene plastic, which makes it robust and virtually maintenance free. More than 46,000 of these boats have been sold internationally, and they are frequently used as a training class in sailing schools. The Topper is 3.4m (11ft 2in) long with a hull weight of 43kg (95 lb), and can also be sailed double-handed. For further details, see the web page www.paw.com/sail/topper

Laser

The Laser, the most widely owned small dinghy, is quick and easy to rig, and simple yet responsive to sail. It is a one-design dinghy class built in GRP by registered builders throughout the world. At 4.3m (13.9ft) long and 59kg (130 lb), the Laser can be rather awkward for one person to move about on land, and sailors need to be at least 75kg (165 lb) to handle it in anything other than a light breeze. However, there is plenty of room to take a friend along for additional weight. More suitable for lighter sailors, but using the same hull, are the Laser Radial and 4.7 rigs, which have smaller sails hoisted on a shorter mast, and are suitable for sailors of 60–70kg (130–155 lb). For more information, see www.lasersailing.com

Splash

The Splash dinghy was designed in the Netherlands. It is a strict one-design class built in GRP. The 3.5m (11ft) Splash is simple to rig and sail, and weighs 55kg (121 lb), so is easy to transport. Also available is the Flash rig, with a longer boom for heavier sailors. For more information, see www.splash-boat.com

THE TOPPER IS A HARDY, LIGHTWEIGHT DINGHY POPULAR WITH BOTH RESORTS AND SAILING SCHOOLS.

ALTHOUGH THE SINGLE-HANDED LASER IS A RELATIVELY SIMPLE DINGHY, IT IS ALSO AN OLYMPIC-CLASS RACER.

MIRRORS, MANY BUILT FROM KITS, ARE POPULAR AS TRAINING DINGHIES.

THE ENTERPRISE, HEAVY FOR ITS SIZE, REMAINS AN EXCITING OPTION.

Double-handed classes
Enterprise

A very popular 4m (13ft 1in) dinghy, suitable for racing and cruising. Boats are now made in fibreglass and composites, as well as the traditional all-timber. The Enterprise has neither spinnaker nor trapeze. Because it is not a light displacement boat, crew weight is not a factor and it can be sailed by two or more sailors. See www.sailenterprise.org.uk

International 420

A one-design class designed in 1959, the 420 is usually known as the 'little sister' of the Olympic Class 470. Widely used as a youth training class, it has a jib and spinnaker, and a trapeze for the crew. It is 4.2m (14ft) long and is designed for a combined crew weight of around 170kg (375 lb). See www.sailingsource.com/420

Laser 2, Laser 2000

Laser produces a range of two-person boats as well as the popular single-hander. The Laser 2 has both jib and spinnaker, but no trapeze. It is 4.37m (14ft 6 in) long and weighs around 73kg (170lb). The Laser 2000 is a newer design aimed at families and beginners and can be sailed by two adults, or two adults with one or two children. It has become the biggest-selling family dinghy in Britain. It is 4.44m long and is made of GRP-foam sandwich, so at 100kg is lighter than many full-fibreglass boats. See www.lasersailing.com

Topper Magno

The Topper Magno is a family sailing boat that can be sailed by two to four people. See www.toppersail-boats.com

Mirror

The Mirror is now one of the most popular one-design dinghies in the world. The 3.3m (10ft 10in) Mirror is frequently used as a youth training boat. See www.ukmirrorsailing.com

How Sailing Works

it is easy to understand how sailing downwind works, with the wind pushing from behind, but how can a boat sail with the wind coming across its side? Why doesn't it simply blow over? What makes it move it forward?

Basic sailing principles

While downwind sails such as spinnakers are designed to present maximum surface area to the wind, utilizing its pushing power, mainsails and jibs are designed to be an aerofoil shape — a curve that will capture wind and channel airflow across them. Because the sail is so thin in section, when it is sitting in line with the wind, the air flows virtually straight past it without providing any power to propel the boat forward.

Trimming

If the boat is at an angle to the wind, and you pull the sail into its aerofoil shape with the mainsheet, the airflow will be disrupted. As you pull the sail on, the airflow will settle down and smooth out on the downwind side as it curves around the back of the sail. The curve on the windward side will then fill with air until the flow is smooth on this side too. When flow is smooth on both sides, the sail is correctly trimmed. This movement of airflow translates into forward movement. On the leeward side of the boat, as the wind curves around the back of the sail to rejoin the airflow across the windward side, it generates a pulling or sucking force.

Sheeting

If the sail is sheeted too hard, there will be no pull, because the airflow across the back of the sail will be turbulent. If the sail is sheeted too loosely, airflow will be disturbed on both sides.

When sailing a two-handed boat, the mainsail and jib should be adjusted in tandem to ensure smooth airflow. If the jib is sheeted incorrectly, the movement of air across its windward surface can cause 'dirty' air to be flicked onto the back of the mainsail.

When the sails are sheeted correctly, and airflow across them is optimized, the boat accelerates. But what is stopping the boat from being pushed sideways? The answer lies in the appendages.

The appendages

The long, flat centreboard sticks down below the bottom of the hull. Like the rudder, it acts as a brake against sideways motion, and helps the boat move forward. Hydrofoils are designed to ensure efficient water flow across their surfaces so they stop the hull from being pushed sideways, but provide little resistance to it moving forward. This further harnesses the wind by channelling its power into forward motion.

The centreboard is partially, then virtually fully, lifted when sailing downwind, because the further you are sailing off the wind, the less of a sideways force is exerted. When sailing dead downwind, the centreboard can be lifted almost entirely out of the water, because it is simply creating drag.

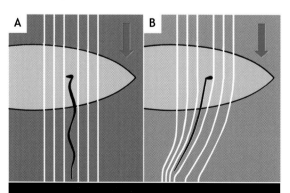

above SAILS OFFER LITTLE RESISTANCE TO WIND (A), UNTIL SHEETED ON (B), WHICH DISRUPTS AIR FLOW AND CREATES A MOTIVE FORCE.

opposite UNDERSTANDING THE PHYSICS OF SAILING MAY INCREASE YOUR ENJOYMENT OF THE SPORT.

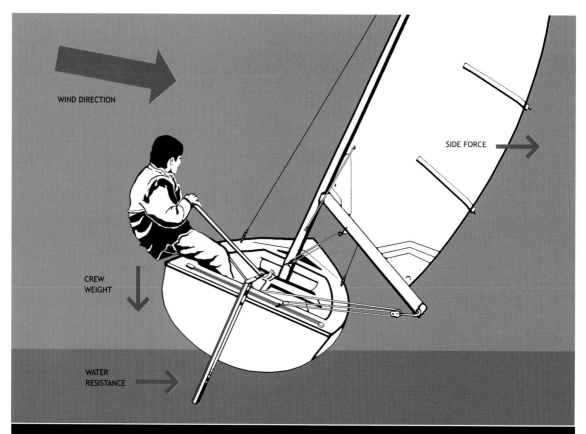

WIND DIRECTION

SIDE FORCE

CREW
WEIGHT

WATER
RESISTANCE

SEVERAL DIFFERENT FORCES MAY BE IN ACTION AT ANY ONE TIME WHILE YOU ARE SAILING. THE SIDEWAYS FORCE OF THE WIND IN THE SAIL IS COUNTERED BY THE HYDROFOILS (RUDDER AND CENTREBOARD). THE WEIGHT OF THE SKIPPER AND CREW WORKS TO KEEP THE BOAT FROM HEELING OVER TOO MUCH, TRANSLATING THE POWER OF THE WIND INTO FORWARD MOTION.

Heeling

Positioned correctly, the weight of the dinghy's crew may also stop it from simply blowing over. The pressure of wind in the sails is countered by the movement of the crew inboard and out. The flatter the boat is sailed, the more the power of the wind can be translated into forward motion. Also, the more the boat heels, the less far down into the water the rudder and centreboard protrude, which increases side slip. The top part of the rudder is exposed as the boat tips over, so it also becomes harder to steer. And finally, the motion of the boat leaning over tends to make the bow round up into the wind. This means that the skipper is constantly pulling the tiller to windward to make the boat bear away again. This is called weather helm, and it can become very tiring!

The tendency for the boat to lean over to leeward, or heel, due to the pressure of the wind in the sails is one aspect of sailing that most often startles beginners to the sport. Because sailing dinghies have little or no built-in ballast, the crew will have to act as a movable weight to keep them from tipping over into the water. Even in light winds, the skipper and crew sit on the windward side of the boat to balance the heeling force of the wind in the sails.

As the wind begins to pick up, the crew will have to hike out — leaning out backwards to get their body weight out over the side of the boat.

Today, most dinghies are fitted with hiking straps or toe straps so the crew can safely tuck their feet or ankles under them and lean out. See also Coping with heel on page 47.

Steering and the rudder

Most sailing dinghies are steered with a transom-hung rudder — a large, flat blade mounted to the back of the boat. This usually has a rounded leading edge and a thin trailing edge, so that it is able to move through the water with relative ease.

Early boats were steered by paddles or oars, combining the actions of steering and propulsion. The modern, vertically-hinged rudder is used to steer the boat by disrupting the flow of water passing off the back of the hull. By angling the blade to the water flow, the stern of the boat is pushed sideways, pivoting around the other underwater appendage, the centreboard or keel.

Attached to the top of the rudder is the tiller, which is used by the skipper to steer. Steering with a rudder is like backing a trailer behind a car, in that it reverses what might seem to be the normal order of things. If you are sitting on the windward side, as you pull the tiller towards you, the rudder angles away, pushing the stern towards you and the bow away. As you push the tiller away, the rudder angles in the opposite direction — towards where you are sitting, pushing the stern away. This way may seem 'backwards' at first, but it soon becomes second nature.

Rudder rules

Because the rudder can only exert its force when water is flowing over it, you can steer only when the boat is moving. Build up speed before trying to change direction.

Because of its size and shape, the rudder can also act as a brake. The harder you push to one side or the other, the more of its surface area is exposed to the water flow, slowing the boat down. Over-steering is not efficient!

For the rudder to be effective in turning the boat, the dinghy needs a central point around which to pivot, so the centreboard needs to be at least partially down before tacking or gybing.

The rudder is most effective when most of it is in the water! If the boat is heeled over too much, the tiller will feel very heavy and the boat will be difficult to steer.

STEERING SKILLS WILL NEED TO BE ACCURATE ONCE YOU START TO RACE USING BUOYS AS TURNING MARKS.

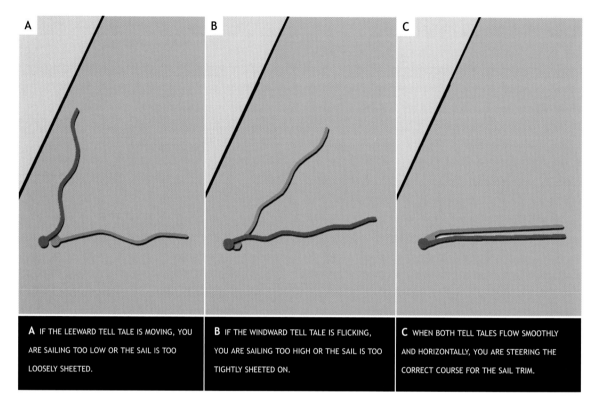

A IF THE LEEWARD TELL TALE IS MOVING, YOU ARE SAILING TOO LOW OR THE SAIL IS TOO LOOSELY SHEETED.

B IF THE WINDWARD TELL TALE IS FLICKING, YOU ARE SAILING TOO HIGH OR THE SAIL IS TOO TIGHTLY SHEETED ON.

C WHEN BOTH TELL TALES FLOW SMOOTHLY AND HORIZONTALLY, YOU ARE STEERING THE CORRECT COURSE FOR THE SAIL TRIM.

Displacement and planing

Most early boats, and many larger ones today, are what are known as displacement boats. A boat's displacement is the weight of water it pushes out of the way when it is floating. The heavier the boat — or the more cargo or people it is carrying — the deeper it will sink into the water. The hulls of displacement boats are thus designed to make the flow of water over them as smooth as possible.

Lighter boats, such as high-performance dinghies and racing powerboats, are designed to skim over the surface of the water, rather than pushing it out of the way as they move forward. This is known as planing.

Most modern dinghies are designed to behave as displacement boats while sailing upwind and at low speeds, but to plane at higher speeds off the wind. Their hulls are fine at the bow, so they can cut through the water efficiently, but with a flattish area aft. As the boat picks up speed, and the crew move their weight aft, only this flat area comes in contact with the water and the boat can skim across the surface. Planing is one of the most thrilling aspects of sailing.

Tell tales

The mainsails and jibs of many boats have tell tales (or woollies) attached to both sides. These short pieces of wool or cotton, with one end stuck to the sail and one end flying free, are positioned to show when the airflow across the sail is smooth. When one or another of them is flicking, airflow is disturbed and the sail is not trimmed efficiently. When they are streaming towards the back of the sail, the sail is correctly trimmed.

If the tell tales on the sail's windward side are flicking, the sail is not trimmed enough. Sheet on the sail until they start to flow. If the leeward tell tales are flicking, the sail is in too tight, so ease it out.

As you will see on pages 45—46, when sailing upwind, the sails are sheeted right in and the skipper steers up or down to keep the tell tales flowing. However, when sailing off the wind, the sails themselves are adjusted to maintain optimum flow. When sailing dead downwind, the tell tales are likely to hang down and look floppy, because you are being pushed along by the wind, rather than harnessing it by directing its flow across the sails.

'True wind' is simply what you feel blowing on your face when you stand still outside and a breeze is blowing. 'Apparent wind' is the stronger breeze you feel when you start walking into it, or the cooling breeze you create if you fan your hand in front of your face. You have created additional airflow through the action of moving.

In this same way, when you are out sailing, it will 'feel' more windy when you are sailing upwind, and less windy when you are sailing downwind. This is because apparent wind is a combination of both the existing, true wind and the speed and direction of the wind caused by the movement of the boat.

For example, if the breeze is eight knots, it will feel as if there is hardly any breeze at all passing across the deck of the boat when you are sailing downwind at six knots. That's because the apparent wind is closer to two knots: the true wind speed less the speed the boat is travelling downwind.

When sailing upwind, the breeze may feel like nine knots, because you are sailing into the eight knots of true wind at, say, four knots of boat speed, on an angle. (If you were powering straight into the breeze in a powerboat, travelling at around 15 knots, the breeze would feel like 23 knots — 8 knots of true wind plus 15 knots created by your movement.)

Apparent wind also blows from a slightly different direction than true wind. Because of the forward motion of the dinghy, apparent wind will always be slightly forward (in other words, more towards the bow of the boat) than the true wind.

This is especially true in the case of extremely fast racing dinghies and multihulls, which are inclined to create so much of their own apparent wind that even when they are simply sailing downwind, the breeze seems to be blowing from their side.

Your tell tales (see page 32), burgee or wind indicator will show the apparent wind direction, which is what you need to sail to.

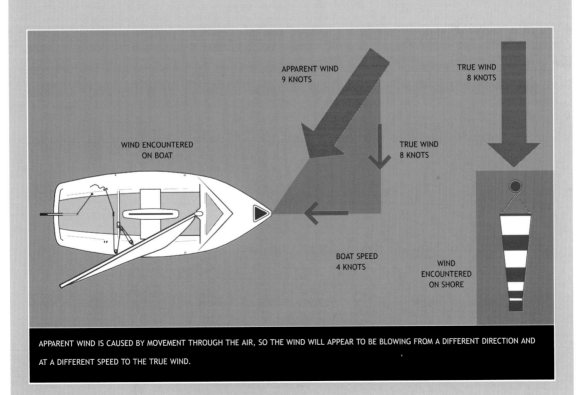

APPARENT WIND
9 KNOTS

TRUE WIND
8 KNOTS

WIND ENCOUNTERED
ON BOAT

TRUE WIND
8 KNOTS

BOAT SPEED
4 KNOTS

WIND
ENCOUNTERED
ON SHORE

APPARENT WIND IS CAUSED BY MOVEMENT THROUGH THE AIR, SO THE WIND WILL APPEAR TO BE BLOWING FROM A DIFFERENT DIRECTION AND AT A DIFFERENT SPEED TO THE TRUE WIND.

Getting Afloat

f you are learning to sail at a sailing school, chances are all you need to do is show up on the beach and your dinghy will be ready for you. However, if you are teaching yourself or training with a friend, you will need to tow or car-top the dinghy to where you are going to sail, and set up, launch and retrieve the boat yourself. Such close interaction with the dinghy will give you a good knowledge of how it works, and how to take care of it.

Trailering and towing

Your boat may come on a road trailer only, or it may have a separate, lightweight beach trailer or launching trolley. Alternatively, it may come with a pair of wheels that clip onto the transom to make it easy to launch and retrieve. The launching trolley may sit on top of the road trailer when the boat is transported, or the boat may have to be lifted onto the lighter trolley once you have reached the launching ramp.

Trailers may have to be registered and certified for use on the road. They should also be insured, and boats insured for trailering, as well as for when on water.

If you are planning to sail in salt water, the road trailer should be galvanized or treated, and the wheel bearings sealed, or it will rust. Like powerboat trailers, many custom-built road trailers for dinghies are designed for immersion, but find out before you try it. Even if the trailer is immersible, it will need to be hosed down with fresh water after each dip.

Your car will need to be able to tow the combined weight of boat and trailer, and to cope with the strain of pulling it out of the water. Many modern dinghies are lightweight so an average-sized car with a 1.6-litre (1600 cc) engine should be suitable. Some smaller, lighter boats can be transported on a car roof-rack, although getting them on and off may require help. Make sure the boat is securely tied down fore and aft, as well as strapped crossways, when transporting by car.

above A LIGHTWEIGHT BEACH TROLLEY WILL MAKE IT EASY TO LAUNCH AND RETRIEVE YOUR DINGHY.

opposite EVEN WHEN SAILING SINGLE-HANDED, YOU WILL NEED SOME HELP GETTING THE DINGHY INTO AND OUT OF THE WATER.

STEP 1 MANOEUVRE THE MAST INTO AN UPRIGHT POSITION BESIDE THE
BOAT. ONE PERSON CAN USE A FOOT AS A BRACE, WHILE THE OTHER
LIFTS THE MAST UPRIGHT.

STEP 2 ONE PERSON CLIMBS INTO THE BOAT AND GUIDES THE BOTTOM,
OR HEEL, OF THE MAST INTO THE FITTING ON THE FLOOR OF THE
DINGHY'S COCKPIT.

STEP 3 CLOSE THE GATE AT DECK LEVEL TO LOCK THE MAST INTO
POSITION, AND THEN ATTACH THE FORE AND SIDESTAYS.

Rigging up

Each boat will have a slightly different rigging system,
from the very simple, such as the Laser, to more complex boats with spinnakers and trapezing systems.
Whatever its type however, if the boat has been trail-
ered or kept in a locker — rather than left fully rigged
in a hard-stand area — you will have to 'step the
mast', securing it in its upright position in the boat.

Many single-handed dinghies such as the Laser have
a simple, two-part mast that simply twists together,
and the sail slides on like a sock. The mast is then
inserted into a hole in the deck, and secured in place
with elastic cord. The vang, outhaul and cunningham
are attached, the mainsheet threaded, and you are
ready to sail!

For boats with stayed masts, such as the 420, the
process is a little more complicated, and requires two
people. One person can lift the mast into position,
while the other attaches the forestay.

Deck-stepped masts

For boats with deck-stepped masts (in other words,
where the base of the mast slots into a fixture at deck
level, forward of the cockpit), the following steps
should be followed:

Step 1 One person holds the mast in a vertical position
beside the boat or on the side deck, parallel to the
mast step on the deck, while the other attaches the
shrouds or sidestays. Alternatively, lay the mast down
on the side decks, with its base next to the mast step.

Step 2 Lift the mast into position, keeping it as vertical as possible, and fit it into the mast step. This will
involve slotting a pin on the bottom of the mast into a
hole — or similar action — to secure it in place.

Step 3 While one person holds the mast in position,
the second person attaches the forestay to the fitting
on the bow.

Keel-stepped masts

For boats on which the mast is keel-stepped (in other
words, the base of the mast slots into a fitting on the
floor of the cockpit, and is then held in place by a gate
at deck level), follow the steps illustrated left.

Hoisting the mainsail

It is easier to hoist the sails on land, while the boat is stable on its trailer. Before hoisting the sails, position the boat so that its bow is pointing into the wind, so the sails do not fill as they are being hoisted.

Hoisting the jib

A jib can be hoisted (see above) before the mainsail. Because it is smaller, and will flap less, it can be put on before launching to enable you to get sailing into deeper water. The mainsail may then be hoisted at sea.

Step 1 Shackle the jib's tack to the fitting on the bow.

Step 2 Shackle the halyard onto the head of the jib. Check that the halyard is not twisted.

Step 3 Pull on the halyard to raise the jib. Position the jib so its leading edge is tight up the forestay. Tie off, cleat or secure the halyard. Tension the halyard so the leading edge of the jib is tight up the forestay.

Step 4 The jib may be attached to the forestay with hanks or domes. Clip these on as the sail is hoisted.

Step 5 Attach the jib sheets to the clew. Thread them through the blocks and lead back into the cockpit.

STEP 1 TO HOIST THE MAINSAIL, PLACE IT IN THE BOTTOM OF THE BOAT. ATTACH THE FOOT OF THE SAIL TO THE BOOM. YOU MAY HAVE TO FEED IT INTO A TRACK RUNNING ALONG THE TOP OF THE BOOM. SECURE THE TACK TO THE FRONT END OF THE BOOM WITH A SHACKLE AND THE CLEW TO THE BACK, USING THE OUTHAUL.

STEP 2 UNROLL THE SAIL IN THE BOTTOM OF THE BOAT. CHECK THAT THE MAIN HALYARD IS NOT TWISTED, BY HOLDING IT AWAY FROM THE BOAT, LOOKING UP ITS LENGTH TO THE TOP OF THE MAST.

STEP 3 INSERT THE BATTENS IN THE SAIL POCKETS.

STEP 4 ATTACH THE HALYARD TO THE HEAD OF THE SAIL. FEED THE TOP OF THE LUFF OR THE SLIDERS ON THIS EDGE OF THE SAIL INTO THE GROOVE RUNNING UP THE MAST, AND TAKE UP THE SLACK ON THE HALYARD.

STEP 5 ONE PERSON FEEDS THE SAIL INTO THE MAST TRACK. THE OTHER PULLS ON THE HALYARD. ONCE HOISTED, ATTACH THE BOOM TO THE MAST AT THE GOOSENECK. TIE OFF, CLEAT OR SECURE THE HALYARD. ATTACH THE VANG AND CUNNINGHAM. THREAD THE MAINSHEET THROUGH THE BLOCKS.

STEP 1 WALK THE DINGHY INTO THE WATER ON ITS BEACH TROLLEY. IF
POSSIBLE, ATTACH A LINE (A PAINTER) TO THE BOW.

STEP 2 ONCE THE BOAT IS FLOATING, PULL THE TROLLEY OUT FROM
UNDERNEATH IT. GET SOMEONE TO HOLD THE BOAT IN PLACE.

STEP 3 WHILE YOUR HELPER TAKES THE TROLLEY ASHORE, MAKE SURE
THAT THE SHEETS ARE RUNNING FREELY SO THAT THE SAILS DON'T
CLEAT THEMSELVES AND FILL WITH WIND.

STEP 4 WHEN RETRIEVING, THE PROCESS IS REVERSED. FLOAT THE BOAT
ONTO THE TROLLEY AND PULL IT OUT OF THE WATER.

Launching and retrieval

Even if you are sailing a single-handed boat, you will
need help when launching and retrieving. Most dinghies
will be on a lightweight trailer or launching trolley,
making it easy to launch them from a beach or ramp.

When moving the boat around on land, especially
over rough ground, make sure you hold onto both the
boat and the trolley. You are more likely to damage the
dinghy's hull while it is on land than once it is afloat.
Be very careful not to scratch or scrape the hull, especially on the trailer, or by dragging its stern on the
ground as you move it up and down slopes.

Before putting the boat in water, ensure the drainage
bung is in place and transom drain holes and self drain-
ers are closed. Many boats will have a ring on the stem
that allows a line (painter) to be attached to the
dinghy's bow. If it is not possible to secure a line, make
it one person's special job to hang onto the boat by its
forestay once it is in the water.

Be prepared to get wet when launching the trolley
into the water, and don't be tempted to push the
dinghy off until it is actually floating. Once you have
succeeded in removing the trolley, stow it somewhere
safe above the high-tide mark.

Most boat ramps are positioned in reasonably sheltered areas, so the boat should be easy to control once
afloat. Keep an eye out for waves. In shallow water —
especially when the beach has shelved up from deeper
water further out — the waves may be quite short and
sharp. The wave pattern will also vary according to
which way the wind is blowing, and how strong it is.

You need to take particular care on a lee shore,
where the wind is blowing onshore. The combined
action of wind and waves will try to push the boat
ashore, and the person holding onto the boat needs to
counter this action.

Retrieving your dinghy

The process of retrieval is exactly the reverse of
launching. One person holds the boat in position, stopping it from running aground, while the other fetches
the trolley. The boat is then floated back onto the trolley, secured to it, and pulled out of the water.

Sailing away from the beach

How you start to sail away from the beach or launching ramp will depend on which way the wind is blowing. It may be a lee shore, a weather shore (where the wind is blowing offshore), or a cross breeze.

Launching from a weather shore

It is easier to launch on a weather shore, as the wind will naturally blow you away from the beach. Give the boat a little push out into the water and then climb aboard. Sheet the sails loosely and steer a reaching course away from the beach.

Launching from a lee shore

On a lee shore, you start off into the wind, and possibly against waves as well. If the wind is not blowing straight onto the beach, and there is room, you may still be able to reach off in one direction or the other.

You will have to give the boat more of a push than you would on a weather shore, and it will be more important to get moving quickly and sailing into deeper water. The skipper will have to sheet the mainsail on rapidly, and the crew get the boat out as far as possible before climbing aboard. They will also have to work quickly to get the centreboard down to stop side slip and the boat being washed back ashore.

Don't try to sail hard on the wind right away — simply concentrate on getting the boat away from the shore and into deeper water.

STEP 1 TURN THE BOAT AROUND SO THE BOW IS FACING OUT TO SEA, AND WALK IT OUT UNTIL THE WATER IS DEEP ENOUGH TO ACCOMMODATE THE RUDDER. INSERT THE CENTREBOARD, PUSHING IT PART-WAY DOWN. IF SAILING A TWO-HANDED DINGHY, THE CREW HOLDS THE BOAT WHILE THE SKIPPER GETS ABOARD AND SORTS OUT THE TILLER AND MAINSHEET. THE CREW THEN PUSHES THE BOAT OFF AND CLIMBS ABOARD.

STEP 2 ON A SINGLE-HANDED BOAT, HOLDING THE MAINSHEET IN ONE HAND AND THE TILLER IN THE OTHER, THE SKIPPER GIVES THE BOAT A GOOD SHOVE OFF AND CLIMBS IN.

STEP 3 START STEERING A REACHING COURSE OUT TO SEA, SHEETING THE SAILS ACCORDINGLY. IN A TWO-HANDED BOAT, SHEET THE JIB FIRST TO MAKE THE BOAT EASIER TO STEER.

Sailing back onto a beach

How you sail back onto the beach is also affected by the wind. If the wind is blowing along the shore, you can simply reach in slowly, let the sails out to slow the boat down, and jump out when the water is shallow enough (remembering to hold onto the boat!).

When returning to a weather shore, tack in to your landing spot, then come head-to-wind at the final stages, letting the wind and power out of the boat's sails. Lift the centreboard before it runs aground.

When coming back onto a lee shore, do not pick up too much speed, and be wary of waves and swell. If possible, before coming right into shore, steer head-to-wind and drop the mainsail, then sail in under jib only.

IF THE WIND IS BLOWING ACROSS THE SHORE, SAIL INTO THE BEACH AND LET THE SAILS RIGHT OUT TO SLOW THE BOAT.

Safety first!

Before heading out onto the water, think about what you want to achieve. You may want to practise a particular skill.

■ The single most important rule is to tell someone when you are going out and when you expect to be back. That way, if you do get into some sort of trouble, someone will know when and where to start looking.

■ Sail with a friend if possible. It will be more fun to share the experience and monitor each other's progress, and will make setting up, launching and retrieval easier.

■ Listen to the weather forecast and check conditions before setting off (see page 74). Err on the side of caution and, if appropriate, check the tide times too.

■ Get to know the area in which you will be sailing, and keep within a reasonably small area when starting out. Make sure you don't sail downwind miles out to sea, and then tire yourself out having to tack all the way back. Know where there might be underwater obstructions, such as rocks and reefs, as well as shipping channels, mooring areas and water-ski lanes.

■ Always wear a well-fitting bouyancy aid!

■ Make sure you have adequate safety equipment, clothing, water and food with you. But above all, remember to have fun.

If this is not possible, sail into the shallow water on a broad reach, then turn head-to-wind. The crew can then jump over the side and hold the boat. Drop the sails at this point if you can, then turn the boat back towards the shore and lift it onto the trolley.

It is very important that the dinghy is not caught stern-on by any large waves. A wave may catch it and slew it around, running it aground and rolling it over, or filling it with water and sand.

If you are sailing single-handed, ask somebody to fetch your trolley for you once you come back to shore. Make sure the centreboard has been lifted right out before the dinghy is put back on its trolley, and then lift or remove the rudder.

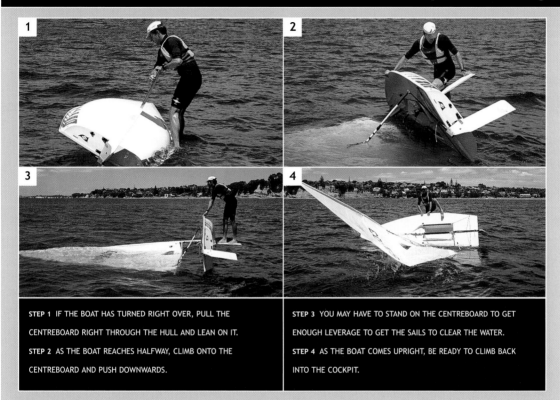

STEP 1 IF THE BOAT HAS TURNED RIGHT OVER, PULL THE CENTREBOARD RIGHT THROUGH THE HULL AND LEAN ON IT.

STEP 2 AS THE BOAT REACHES HALFWAY, CLIMB ONTO THE CENTREBOARD AND PUSH DOWNWARDS.

STEP 3 YOU MAY HAVE TO STAND ON THE CENTREBOARD TO GET ENOUGH LEVERAGE TO GET THE SAILS TO CLEAR THE WATER.

STEP 4 AS THE BOAT COMES UPRIGHT, BE READY TO CLIMB BACK INTO THE COCKPIT.

Sooner or later, the dinghy will turn over on its side and capsize. This is a normal side-effect of the principles of physics involved in sailing. You may want to practise dealing with a situation in which your dinghy capsizes, but this should always be done in safe, gentle waters, where there is help nearby.

Capsizes occur for several reasons, and the boat can roll to leeward or to windward. You may capsize to leeward if the boat is overpowered and heels over too much. If the end of the boom hits the water, it is usually all over. You may also capsize to leeward if one of the boat's fittings breaks suddenly, especially if a hiking strap comes loose.

Capsizes to windward may occur if the helmsman lets go of the tiller or the mainsheet, or there is a sudden lull – all of which may cause the boat to suddenly come upright. Bearing away too suddenly or letting the mainsail out too far on a run may also cause a sudden capsize, as can broaching when sailing under spinnaker (see page 61).

Saving the situation

It is usually fairly easy to right the boat after a leeward capsize, as you should fall or be able to climb clear of the hull. After a capsize to windward, you may have to swim out from under the sails as the boat has effectively fallen over on top of you.

Use the centreboard as leverage to right the boat by standing up or crouching down on it near to where it comes out of the hull. On double-handed boats, pull on the windward jib sheet as the boat comes upright. Once the mainsail is out of the water, the boat may right quickly, so be ready to scramble aboard.

If the boat turns right over so that the mast is facing vertically downwards, it will be much more difficult to return to the upright position. Pull the centreboard right through the hull, using your weight as leverage (and the jib sheet on a double-handed boat) to bring the boat onto its side, and then right it as explained above.

Sailing into the Wind

now that you are on the water, it's time to start sailing. Depending on where you have launched your boat and the wind direction, the easiest point of sailing with which to start is probably a beam reach, sailing on an angle of around 90° to the wind.

The tendency of a sailing dinghy, when its sails are not sheeted on and there is no particular tide or current, is to sit head-to-wind. Its bow will point straight into the breeze and the sail will flap gently. This offers the least possible resistance to the breeze, which flows evenly down each side of the sail.

If you pull the tiller towards you and pull on the mainsheet a little, the bow will move away from pointing into the wind and airflow will begin to move across the sail, creating power and allowing the dinghy to accelerate. You will feel the pressure of both the wind in the sail and the water moving across the surface of the rudder, through the tiller.

As the dinghy picks up speed and power, it may start to heel. Steer further away from the wind (by pulling the tiller towards you) — which will lessen the angle of wind across the sail — or ease the mainsheet, which has the same effect by spilling air and power out of the sail. The boat should 'flatten out' and slow down, at which point you can start experimenting again, pulling on the mainsail and bringing the dinghy's bow further up into the wind by pushing the tiller away from you.

You will soon find a point at which the dinghy is moving smoothly, with a comfortable amount of heel. You will also be able to feel the weight of the rudder on the tiller, but it should not feel heavy to steer. As the wind fluctuates in strength and direction, you can adjust your course with the tiller, or the trim of the sails.

But you can't keep sailing along on a reach forever! Depending on the wind direction, you will probably have to sail upwind at some point.

Harnessing the wind

Trimming is the action of pulling the ropes attached to the sails to change the sail shape and harness the wind. These ropes are called sheets, so the action of pulling them in is called 'sheeting' or 'trimming'. The opposite of trimming is 'easing', when the sheets are let out. Sails are said to be correctly trimmed when they are adjusted for maximum efficiency and air flow. See Tell tales on page 32.

above A SUDDEN GUST WILL CAUSE THE DINGHY TO HEEL. TO FLATTEN OUT, YOU WILL NEED TO EASE THE MAINSHEET OR LUFF UP.

opposite DINGHY RACES GENERALLY START WITH AN UPWIND LEG, WITH BOATS BEATING TO THE FIRST MARK.

On the wind

Sailing with the boat on an angle as close to the wind direction as possible has many names: beating, sailing to windward or upwind, sailing hard-on or close-hauled. Your course, when sailing on the wind, is divided into two tacks or boards: starboard (when the wind is coming over the starboard tack side of the boat) and port tack (when the wind is coming over the port side).

ALTHOUGH DIFFERENT BOATS FOLLOW DIFFERENT ZIGZAG COURSES, THEY END UP AT THE SAME WINDWARD POINT.

Changing between these two courses to gain ground to windward — by pushing the bow of the boat through the eye of the wind (the direction from which it is blowing) — is called tacking or 'going about'. Zigzagging from one close-hauled course to the other is the only way to sail in a windward direction. It is not possible to sail straight into the wind, because you need the wind to move over the sailin order to power the boat forwards.

Historically, ships had their sails rigged athwartships — at right angles to the boat's centreline — and could only really sail downwind. Making ground to windward was a slow and tedious process of zigzagging back and forth on a very wide angle. Boats would frequently be stuck in bays or have to turn a number of times to clear a point. They were truly at the mercy of the wind in terms of where they wanted to go.

These early vessels couldn't tack either, sending their bow though the eye of the wind; they had to 'wear ship', meaning turning their wide sails and even wider sterns away from the breeze so the wind moved around behind them — the ancestor of today's gybe — each time losing ground to leeward.

Modern yachts are, however, designed to sail as close as 35° to the apparent wind. This means they have a tacking angle (the angle between their course relative to the wind on port and starboard tacks) of around 80° between tacks, allowing for the true wind. It still means zigzagging if you want to go in an upwind direction, but today's yachts are easier to control and much more efficient sailing on the wind.

Sailing upwind is not as simple as just reaching along, because it involves sailing along a fine, invisible line, demarcating the closest your boat can sail to the wind direction. Of course, if you are just out for a day sail, having a good time, and not trying to reach any particular point, then it doesn't matter if you don't sail as close to the wind as possible or have the sails trimmed as efficiently as you could. However, if you do want to make serious ground to windward, or if you ever want to race, you have to learn how to make the boat sail as high as possible — as close to the wind as its design and your sails and crew weight allow.

TO COME UP INTO THE WIND, PULL THE MAINSHEET FULLY ON, AND PUSH THE TILLER AWAY FROM YOU UNTIL THE LEADING EDGE OF THE MAINSAIL STARTS TO FLAP. BEAR AWAY A LITTLE AND YOU ARE ON THE OPTIMUM ON-THE-WIND COURSE.

Coming onto the wind

When reaching, start coming up onto the wind by pushing the tiller gently away from you. The bow will swing around towards the direction of the wind.

If you do this without also pulling in the sheets, the boat will slow down and eventually come to a stop. If you push the tiller far enough, you will end up sitting head-to-wind, sails flapping. This is called 'heaving to', but you do not want to be in this position when you are trying to sail on the wind, and you certainly don't want to end up 'in irons'. This is when you are sitting head-to-wind and the dinghy is not moving. You have no steering power and the boat may start to move backwards — onto the shore or onto another boat!

To get out of irons, use the sails to steer the dinghy back into a position where they can pick up the breeze. Push the boom out to the side of the dinghy so that the mainsail is at right angles to the wind (this is called 'backing the main'). At the same time, push the tiller toward the boom (so the rudder is on the opposite angle to the sail). The boat will begin to turn and move backwards and, once you have steerage, you will start sailing again.

IF YOU COME UP TOO HIGH AND FIND YOURSELF SITTING HEAD-TO-WIND, PUSH OUT THE BOOM TO BACK THE MAIN. PUSH THE TILLER TOWARDS THE BOOM TO REGAIN YOUR STEERAGE.

From a reach, push the tiller away from you slowly and gradually, bringing the mainsheet on as you do so. The wind indicator and tell tales will show you how close you are sailing to the wind. Pull the mainsheet and jib sheets as far in as you can. As you get closer to sailing on the wind, the boat may start to heel over as it powers up, so adjust your body weight and hike out accordingly. Try to keep the boat as flat as possible.

With the sails fully sheeted, push the tiller away until the front edges of the sails start to flap. This shows that the wind is now blowing across the back, rather than over their windward side. When this happens, you are sailing too close to the wind (this is called pinching), so bear away a little by pulling the tiller towards you. If sailing a two-handed boat, watch the front edge and tell tales of the jib. If sailing a single-handed yacht with a main only, watch the front edge of the main.

The tell tales will have gone through a series of movements (see page 32). As you are coming up into the wind, the tell tales on the sail's leeward side will move about. You will then reach a point where both the windward and leeward tell tales are flowing properly. This is the optimum on-the-wind position, with airflow even and efficient on both sides of the sail. If you keep coming up, the windward tell tales will start to flicker, as you have sailed too high (too close to the wind) and airflow across the sail is no longer efficient. Bear away slightly until you have good flow on the tell tales.

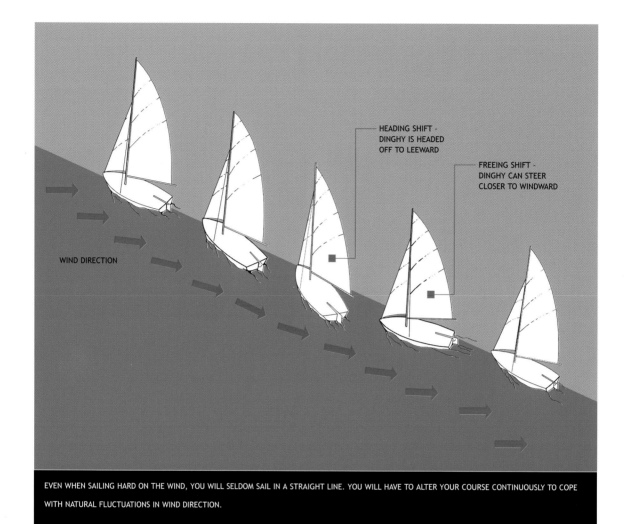

HEADING SHIFT -
DINGHY IS HEADED
OFF TO LEEWARD

FREEING SHIFT -
DINGHY CAN STEER
CLOSER TO WINDWARD

WIND DIRECTION

EVEN WHEN SAILING HARD ON THE WIND, YOU WILL SELDOM SAIL IN A STRAIGHT LINE. YOU WILL HAVE TO ALTER YOUR COURSE CONTINUOUSLY TO COPE WITH NATURAL FLUCTUATIONS IN WIND DIRECTION.

Wind shifts

Of course, it would be easy to sail on the wind if all you had to do was find this magical line — not too high and not too low — and steer straight along it. However, the air is always moving, and the wind is never constant. Firstly, it rises and falls in strength (see Seeing the wind on page 48) and, secondly, it fluctuates in direction — sometimes only slightly, sometimes by 10° or more. These movements are called wind shifts.

When a wind shift enables you to sail higher — closer to the direction from which the breeze was originally blowing — it is called a lift or freeing shift. When it forces you to steer a course down and away from the direction in which you were sailing, it is called a knock or heading shift.

Watch your tell tales and the sails all the time, as the wind lifts and knocks. To adjust to this, tiller movements should be gentle and gradual, a little at a time, so you do not disrupt the sailing action of the boat.

When the wind is lifting, your leeward tell tales will flicker, indicating that you can steer higher. Likewise, in a knock, the windward tell tales will start to move around, and the sails may start to back, as if you are sailing too high up into the wind or pinching (which in effect, you are, as the wind has moved around you).

You will quickly learn to keep the boat 'in the groove', adjusting your course as the wind fluctuates. When you are steering the correct course, with the sails trimmed, the boat will feel balanced and powered up, and there should be little weight on the helm.

Coping with heel

To cope with fluctuations in the strength of the breeze, adjust your body position and maybe even your sail trim and course, or the dinghy will heel over as more wind exerts pressure on the sails. You can, however, counter the heeling action in several ways:

■ **De-powering** Simply de-power the dinghy by easing out the mainsail. This lets the air out of the sail, and the boat will flatten out. This, however, is rather inefficient because you have effectively 'turned off' the dinghy's power. If you do this regularly, the boat will alternate between heeling over and speeding up, flattening out and slowing down.

In stronger breezes, easing the main is the sensible option — or you risk capsizing. In a two-handed boat, ease the main first, and the jib only in strong breezes. This helps you sail hard on the wind; you will lose your upwind course if you let it go too much.

■ **Body weight** The second option is to use your body weight to bring the boat upright. Hiking out a little — or a lot, depending on the gust — should allow the dinghy to become more upright. Move inboard again when the breeze lightens, or the boat may tip over to windward! How much you can use your body weight to counter the wind will, however, depend on the type of dinghy, its size, shape, and the combined weight of you and your crew.

■ **Pinching and feathering** Pinching is sailing too close to the wind, above the invisible line, so that airflow across the sails becomes inefficient. In the same way you would luff up hard to come head-to-wind and stop, this simply de-powers the boat and flattens it out without losing ground to leeward. Pinching and steering back down repeatedly as the gusts hit is called feathering because the movements are small. You steer up a little and down a little as the wind strength rises and falls — an important technique when you have to make as much ground to windward as possible.

When feathering, be ready to ease the main if you still find yourself over-powered. If you feel the rudder begin to load up, and the helm becomes heavy, let out the mainsheet — or you may lose steerage and capsize.

You will probably use a combination of all three techniques to keep the boat flat when sailing upwind, depending on wind and wave conditions, and how committed you are to sailing truly upwind. The closer you sail to the wind without pinching, the less distance you will have to cover if you are aiming for a point directly to windward — particularly common in competitive racing.

HAVING JUST CHANGED TACK, THE HELMSMAN WILL NEED TO FINE-TUNE THE RIG AND REPOSITION BODY WEIGHT TO KEEP THE BOAT AS FLAT AS POSSIBLE.

Increases in the strength of the breeze are called puffs or gusts, and areas of less wind are called lulls. You may hear racing sailors refer to increases and decreases in pressure, or to the breeze building and lightening off. When there is little breeze, the weather conditions are said to be light, and when it is windy, conditions are heavy.

Sometimes the puffs and lulls of the breeze may seem to follow a pattern, sometimes they will be random. It is in the nature of the wind to fluctuate, plus it will also be affected by the geography of where you are sailing. For example, a breeze may funnel down onto the water out of a valley, causing a river of wind, or you may sail out of the shelter of a headland into more open water and a stronger breeze.

With practice, you can learn to see how the wind is fluctuating by watching its effects on the water. Try watching the surface of the sea or lake before going out for a sail, maybe from a jetty or headland, where you can look down on it. Apart from the waves, you should be able to see darker and lighter patches on the water, which indicate areas of different wind strength. The darker patches are caused by greater amounts of breeze ruffling the surface of the water. Especially on days with only a light breeze, you may be able to see discrete patches of wind and watch them move across the water. You will soon learn to look around you while sailing and gauge whether you are sailing into an area of more or less wind, or if a gust is moving towards you across the surface of the water.

TO AVOID LULLS (AREAS OF LITTLE OR NO WIND), THE HELMSMAN WILL NEED TO KEEP A WATCHFUL EYE ON THE WATER, WHERE DARKER PATCHES OF SHADOW WILL INDICATE AREAS OF MORE WIND.

Changing direction

It is all very well to get the hang of sailing along on the wind — 'in the groove' — but what happens if you cannot sail directly to where you want to go in a straight line, or if your intended destination is to windward? What if there is a geographical feature, an anchored boat, or another sailing dinghy in the water and you need to avoid it by sailing to windward?

As we mentioned earlier, it is impossible to sail straight into the wind. You will have to tack, or beat, to get where you are going. This is where the zigzagging comes in. You will have to change direction by steering the dinghy's bow through the eye of the wind and out onto the other side, so that the wind is blowing over your other shoulder — that is, onto the opposite tack.

Tacking, or 'going about', is the easiest way to change from one tack to the other. It is also possible to do this by gybing (see also Chapter 7: Sailing off the wind on page 54). Using this particular technique, the back of the dinghy — and, therefore, the trailing edge of the main — passes through the eye of the wind, but this is practical only when you are sailing off the wind.

Going from tack to tack through the eye of the wind means that the bow of the dinghy passes through an arc of only about 80° — from an angle of 40° to the wind on one tack to 40° off the wind on the other. If you were to gybe around, it would mean circling the other way, so the bow would pass through 280°.

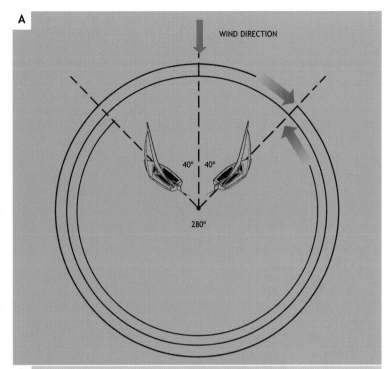

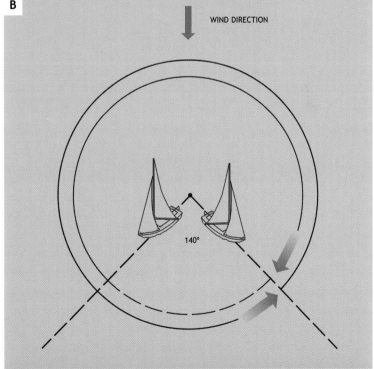

A TACKING FROM BEAT TO BEAT MEANS THAT THE DINGHY DOES A 80° TURN, WHILE GYBING FROM BEAT TO BEAT MEANS THAT THE DINGHY DOES A 270° TURN.

B GYBING FROM REACH TO REACH MEANS THAT THE DINGHY GOES THROUGH A 140° TURN.

STEP 1 AS YOU ARE SAILING ALONG ON THE WIND, BE SURE TO CHECK THAT THE WATER INTO WHICH YOU WILL BE TACKING IS ENTIRELY CLEAR OF ANY OBSTRUCTIONS.

STEP 2 PUSH THE TILLER AWAY FROM YOU IN ORDER TO PUSH THE BOAT'S BOW UP INTO THE EYE OF THE WIND.

STEP 3 THE BOOM WILL COME ACROSS THE BOAT'S CENTRELINE AS THE WIND STARTS TO COME ACROSS THE OTHER SIDE OF THE SAIL. DUCK UNDER THE BOOM, KEEPING THE TILLER OVER UNTIL THE TACK IS COMPLETE.

STEP 4 MOVE ACROSS TO THE NEW WINDWARD SIDE, AND CENTRE THE TILLER TO GET THE BOAT SAILING ON THE NEW TACK.

Tacking

Tacking is very simple. Firstly, if you are sailing a two-handed dinghy, tell the crew that you want to tack, so that they can prepare. Look over your shoulder and work out roughly where you will be steering when you come out of the tack — about 70° or 80° from the course you are currently sailing. You may become disoriented and not be able to work out where you should be steering once you complete the tack, so be prepared.

To start the tack, while sailing along on the wind and sitting to windward, push the tiller away from you to turn the dinghy's bow into the wind. Start slowly and gently, and then increase the speed and pressure as the dinghy comes head-to-wind. Every boat will respond differently, but push just enough to bring the bow right up into the wind and out the other side. If you don't push the tiller far enough, you will end up stopping head-to-wind, with the risk of ending up in irons. If you push too hard, the boat will swing around too quickly, and you may lose your balance and your bearings. If you push the tiller too hard and too far over, the rudder will effectively act as a brake because the blade will be at a sharp angle to the water flow, and you will lose speed. Practise how far and fast you have to push the tiller to get the boat to move smoothly and at the right speed through the tack.

Once you have completed the tack, head on your new course and watch your wind indicator, sails and tell tales to get back on the wind on this new tack. Remember to bring the tiller back to the centreline and check that you are happy with the course you are now steering. If you hold the tiller over for too long as you tack, you run the risk of coming out of the tack too low — on a close reach, rather than on the wind. It is better, however, to go too far — and then come back up on the wind once you have settled on the new tack — than not go far enough around, and lose speed and momentum by coming out too high.

At the same time as you push the tiller across, ease the mainsail slightly. This will increase airflow across the sail and give you some speed coming out the other side of the tack. Once you have completed the tack and have come on the wind on the opposite board, bring the mainsheet back on.

How you swap sides to get to the new windward side will vary from boat to boat, according to how much room you have to manoeuvre, but keep low so that the boom does not hit you as it comes across, and try to remain facing forwards. You are more likely to be disoriented if you stop looking where you are going.

Start to move across as you push the tiller away, crossing the centreline only when the boom has reached the centre. As you move across, swap the hands which are operating the tiller and mainsheet. Even though most people are right-handed, all sailors have to be ambidextrous in this respect: you always steer with your inboard or aft hand, and trim with the other. Depending on the style of tiller, you should be able to pass it around behind yourself, and swap hands as you step across. If you are using a tiller extension, either shorten it down (if it is the telescopic type), or fold it partially back on itself as you tack.

WHEN TACKING A TWO-HANDED DINGHY, THE CREW CROSSES THE CENTRELINE AND SHEETS THE JIB ON THE NEW LEEWARD SIDE.

Tacking tips

You may have to tack to move around an obstacle but, generally, you can tack at any time – as long as there is clear water.

A few simple points should determine the timing of your tack:

■ **Speed** Having some speed up when going into the tack will give you the momentum you need to carry the dinghy through the manoeuvre. You do not want to end up in irons, heading straight up into the wind with no forward way. Make sure that you are sailing efficiently, with the main trimmed, providing plenty of power. If necessary, bear away slightly to increase speed before tacking. There also has to be water flowing over the rudder for your tiller movements to have any effect. If you are not moving, you can push the tiller over as hard as you like, and nothing will happen...

■ **Waves** If possible, wait for reasonably flat water in which to tack. Tacking in waves can slow down or even stop the dinghy. Look out ahead of you for a gap between waves, or an area where the waves are smaller.

■ **Obstacles** Make sure you have clear water in which to tack. Check that you will not be crossing the course of another boat and that there is no obstacle with which you will collide when you start sailing on a course about 80° or 90° to the one you are currently on. Remember the 'rules of road at sea' (see pages 82–83): if you are tacking onto port, for example, you will not have priority when you cross the path of another boat on the starboard tack.

■ **Wind** If you need to gain ground to windward – especially if you start racing – tack when the breeze is knocking you. When the wind is heading, it forces you to sail further away from your destination on the tack you are on. However, if you go about onto the other tack, you will be able to sail closer to your goal. Inversely, if you tack on a lift – when the wind direction is allowing you to sail more directly to your goal – you will be headed on the other tack.

ALWAYS MAKE SURE YOU ARE TACKING INTO CLEAR WATER, AND NOT INTO THE PATH OF OTHER BOATS.

TRY TO FACE FORWARD THROUGHOUT THE TACK SO THAT YOU DO NOT BECOME DISORIENTED.

YOU WILL NEED TO BE ABLE TO USE BOTH HANDS, AND PRACTISE SWAPPING YOUR MAINSHEET AND TILLER HANDS.

Roll tacking is commonly used in racing to help smooth out tacks in light weather. Think of it as rolling the boat around a curved corner, rather than making a hard, angular turn. This enables the dinghy to roll around onto the new tack without losing momentum, and can even help you accelerate out of your tacks.

To start the roll tack, allow the dinghy to heel to leeward and then lean out hard to windward before pushing the tiller across. This should roll the boat slightly to windward as it starts to turn — but don't lean out too far, or you will almost certainly overbalance and capsize to windward! Leaning the boat over to windward will point the bow up into the wind, hastening the tack. This is especially important if you are sailing in very light conditions, when it can be difficult to gather enough momentum to tack.

When you are just about to get your bottom wet, cross smartly to the other side and hike out hard to flatten the boat out. This will help you to accelerate out of the tack — important in light conditions — as it will cause airflow across the sails.

This is a technique that requires practice and the ability to 'get in the groove', but once you've mastered it, it will be a breeze — but be prepared to fall overboard a few times!

STEP 1 IN LIGHT WINDS AND FLAT WATER, IT CAN BE AN ADVANTAGE TO ROLL THE DINGHY THROUGH THE TACK.

STEP 2 ALLOW THE BOAT TO HEEL TO LEEWARD, THEN LEAN OUT HARD TO WINDWARD BEFORE PUSHING THE TILLER AWAY FROM YOU. THIS WILL MAKE THE BOW ROUND UP INTO THE WIND.

STEP 3 PUSH THE BOAT THROUGH THE TACK, STAYING ON THE OLD WINDWARD SIDE AS IT CURVES AROUND THE CORNER.

STEP 4 JUST AS YOU ARE ABOUT TO GET YOUR BOTTOM WET, CROSS TO THE OTHER SIDE AND HIKE HARD OUT TO WINDWARD TO FLATTEN THE BOAT OUT, MAKING IT ACCELERATE OUT OF THE TACK.

Sailing off the Wind

reaching is probably the easiest and most comfortable point of sail. You can set off from the beach and simply cruise along with the sails loosely sheeted, without too much effort or heel.

Any point of sail — the angle to the wind at which a boat is sailing — that is not on the wind is called 'sailing off the wind', 'sailing downwind' or 'reaching'. Sailing directly downwind — with the wind coming straight over the stern — is called 'running' or 'sailing flat-off'.

As a general rule on a dead run, the further off the wind you are sailing, the further out the sails should be. Watch your wind indicator, and try to keep the boom at a 90° angle to the direction from which the wind is blowing. Also watch your tell tales, and try to keep them streaming, obeying the same principles as when sailing upwind. However, instead of altering your course to keep them flowing — steering up when the leeward tell tales are flicking, and down if the windward ones

are flicking — adjust your sails instead. Sheet on the main or jib if the leeward tell tales are moving about, and let them out if the windward ones start to flick. To find the best sail position, ease the sails out until they start to luff, then bring them back in slightly.

Unless you are racing, or need to sail at a certain angle to avoid an obstacle, you can probably steer wherever you want. Because there is no 'invisible line' along which to sail — as there is when you are sailing to windward — you can choose a point in the distance (an island, lighthouse or tall building on shore) and steer for it. Adjust the sails to keep the boat flat, rather than alter course to keep the boat 'in the groove'. As the wind fluctuates in strength and direction, move your body weight inboard and out. Use your heading (the point you have identified in the distance) as a guide to where to steer, rather than the shape of the sails or the movement of tell tales.

above and opposite OFF THE WIND IS A FAST AND EXCITING POINT OF SAIL. MANY DINGHY CLASSES CARRY SPECIAL DOWNWIND SAILS — SPINNAKERS AND GENNAKERS — TO MAKE THE RIDE FASTER AND MORE EXCITING.

Maintaining your course

If you want to maintain the course you are sailing — if, for example, you need to avoid an obstacle such as a headland — on a windy day, try to sail higher when the wind lightens off. There will be less pressure on the sails, and you will be able to sail on a tighter reach without the boat heeling over too much. Sail high while you can and then, when gusts hit, you can bear away to de-power without ending up much lower than your original course. You will sail in an undulating zigzag pattern, with your intended course running more or less down the middle.

As with sailing upwind, you will soon be able to feel when the boat is trimmed correctly and the sails are working efficiently. Practise letting the sails in and out and steering up and down to find the right groove for the wind and wave conditions.

De-powering

There are several ways to de-power (see Coping with heel on page 47) and reduce heeling when reaching.

When sailing upwind, you can de-power by pinching — steering the boat up into the wind to reduce the power generated by the sails. When sailing off the wind, the opposite is true. If you come up (see Reaching on page 57), you are effectively putting the boat on a tighter reach, and it will accelerate. Instead, bear away when the wind strength increases, and the boat will flatten off and de-power as less wind flows across the sails. Always ease out the sails as you are bearing away.

As you would when sailing upwind, you can use your body weight to keep the boat flat, hiking out to windward when the boat heels over, and moving back inboard when it lightens off. Sail the boat as flat as possible.

It is also important when sailing downwind to move your body weight fore and aft. In windy conditions, and when the boat is moving quickly through the water, move your weight aft to lift the bow out of the water and help the dinghy plane (see Displacement and planing on page 32). In lighter conditions, move forward so that the flatter, fatter sections of the dinghy lift out of the water, reducing drag.

PRIOR TO THE START OF A RACE, COMPETITORS CONTINUALLY DE-POWER BY PINCHING TO ENABLE THEM TO ATTAIN THE BEST STARTING POSITION ON THE LINE WITHOUT OVERSHOOTING THE MARK BEFORE THE GUN GOES OFF.

WHEN SAILING A LONG WAY OFF THE WIND, THE DINGHY SHOULD SIT QUITE FLAT ON THE WATER AND TRIMMING WILL BE EASY.

Reaching

Steering the boat onto an on-the-wind course (see Coming onto the wind on page 45) involves 'coming up' — pushing the tiller away from you to send the bow up into the wind, and bringing the sheets hard in. Moving from an on-the-wind course onto a reach involves bearing away — pulling the tiller towards you so that the bow moves away from the wind direction, coupled with an easing of the sheets. The more you bear away, the broader the reach on which you sail.

A course slightly off the wind — that is, just below that invisible line above which the boat will not sail — with the sheets slightly eased, is called a 'tight reach' or 'close reach'. On a two-handed or larger dinghy that carries a spinnaker, a reach that is not far enough off the wind to allow this sail to be hoisted is called a 'two-sail reach', because you are still sailing along on the power of the jib and main working together.

On a tight reach, the slightly eased sails often generate quite a lot of power, which you can control by easing them out. By and large, you would only use tight reaching in racing situations, where you have to sail to a certain mark, or if you feel the need for speed.

Bearing away slightly from hard on the wind and easing the sheets will cause the boat to accelerate in most breezes, and give you an exhilarating ride.

Trim and balance are both important on this point of sail, to maintain power and speed. You will have to respond closely to the strength and directional fluctuations of the breeze, sheeting and coming up to gain more power as the wind drops away, and bearing away and easing out the sheets when the gusts hit.

Bearing further away — so that the wind is blowing across the boat at a 90° angle — your course is called a beam reach. This is a comfortable, easy point of sail. The boat should be quite flat, and you can control overpowering by easing the sails and hiking.

If you are sailing even further away from the wind — between 100° and 170° to the wind — you are on a 'broad reach'. This will be slower than tight or beam reaching, but very comfortable — just cruising along with the sails well eased. The dinghy should be sitting very flat on the water and, unless it is very windy, should not become overpowered or heel over. If you are hit by a gust, simply ease the sheets or steer further downwind and run with it.

Running

If you are sailing dead downwind, with the wind blowing over the stern, the mainsail should be eased out as far as it can go, round to the side stays holding the mast in place, so that you are just being pushed by the wind.

Some sailing dinghies, such as Lasers, when running dead downwind, sail better with a little windward heel because of their hull shape. Sit to windward and try to tip the dinghy slightly that way – but don't lean it too far or you may roll to windward and end up in the water!

When sailing flat-off, due to fluctuations in wind direction or your steering, the wind may approach from beyond 90° to the beam – that is, over the leeward stern quarter. This is called 'sailing by the lee', and is rather dangerous. If the wind shifts further, it may start to blow around the front side of your eased-out mainsail, and force it to flick across to the other side of the boat, sometimes with great force – an accidental gybe. This can cause you to capsize.

If you find that you are sailing by the lee, steer up slightly so the wind angle is coming more from aft, or over the windward stern quarter. This will avoid the possibility of an unwanted and unexpected gybe.

Downwind sails

When sailing downwind, the dinghy is powered mostly by the push of the wind, so increasing the sail area will increase power. To do this, some two-handed and larger boats have an extra sail (spinnaker or gennaker), which is hoisted when sailing downwind. A gennaker, however, can be used to sail on tighter reaches for a faster, more exciting ride. You cannot sail dead downwind under gennaker, instead sailing a zigzag course.

If your dinghy does not have a spinnaker, you should utilize the jib's surface area. When the jib is sheeted on the leeward side, it is blanketed by the mainsail. The jib needs to be sheeted to windward, so that its surface is exposed to the wind on the opposite side to the main. This is called sailing 'wing-and-wing'.

On small boats, in light weather, you should be able to pull the jib around using the windward sheet, and either hold the clew to windward or cleat it off. On larger boats, and those with spinnakers, you may need to use the spinnaker pole or a whisker pole to hold out the clew. Run the windward jib sheet through the pole's outboard end and extend it out to windward, clipping the butt of the pole onto the mast. Pull on the jib sheet until the clew of the sail is at the end of the pole.

STEP 1 SAILING DEAD DOWNWIND, WITH THE MAINSAIL AT RIGHT ANGLES TO THE CENTRELINE, USE YOUR WEIGHT TO MAKE THE BOAT SIT FLAT.

STEP 2 LEAN SLIGHTLY TO WINDWARD TO GIVE THE HULL A LITTLE HEEL.

WHEN ON TIGHTER REACHES, YOU MAY STILL HAVE TO HIKE TO KEEP THE BOAT FLAT. AS WHEN SAILING UPWIND, LEAN IN AND OUT TO KEEP THE BOAT UPRIGHT AS GUSTS HIT.

TO GYBE, SIMPLY STEER THE BOAT FURTHER AND FURTHER OFF THE WIND UNTIL THE STERN AND BACK EDGE OF THE MAINSAIL PASS THROUGH THE EYE OF THE WIND. THE MAIN THEN COMES ACROSS THE CENTRELINE, AND YOU ARE AWAY ON THE NEW GYBE.

Gybing

There will come a time when sailing downwind when you will need to change direction. Sailing dead downwind can be a bit slow, and you might prefer to sail a zigzag course downwind, going from reach to exciting reach, instead of running flat-off.

Just as you can tack to change direction when sailing upwind, with the bow of the boat passing through the eye of the wind, you can also tack from reach to reach. For example, if you are on a tight reach, with the sheets only slightly eased from hard-on, it is easy to steer up to an on-the-wind course and then tack onto the opposite reach.

But what if you are broad reaching on an angle of 160° to the wind, and want to reach off to about the same angle with the wind coming from the other side? It would be quicker for the bow to pass through the 40° between these two angles, with the stern passing through the eye of the wind. You then need to gybe.

Gybing occurs when the stern of the boat passes through the eye of the wind. Instead of the leading edge of the mainsail passing through the head-to-wind position and the breeze swapping smoothly from one side of the sail to the other, gybing is a sudden movement. The wind direction moves quickly from one side to the other of the trailing edge of the mainsail, flicking it over.

You need to be able to control this manoeuvre for a number of reasons:
■ the main may come across too quickly and throw the dinghy off balance, resulting in a capsize;
■ the swiftly moving boom may hit the skipper or crew on the head as it swings across with force, even in relatively light conditions;
■ the boat powers up as soon as the gybe is complete, because the flat surfaces of the sails are exposed to the wind.

While you are still learning to sail, and on windy days while you are still gaining your skills and confidence, you might like to tack around downwind, even if it does mean going almost full circle. This is the safest and easiest procedure if you want to avoid capsizing. It is also the best way of changing direction when tight reaching. Steer the dinghy up to an on-the-wind course before tacking, however, so that you have enough momentum to get you through it.

STEP 1 WITH THE DINGHY CORRECTLY TRIMMED AND BALANCED, YOU SHOULD LOWER THE CENTREBOARD PART OF THE WAY TO ENSURE ADDITIONAL STABILITY.

STEP 2 PULL THE TILLER TOWARDS YOU. CONTROL THE MAINSAIL, USING THE THE SHEET AS IT CROSSES THE BOAT, AND KEEP YOUR HEAD CLEAR OF THE BOOM.

STEP 3 MOVE ACROSS THE BOAT, MAKING SURE THAT YOU DON'T SHEET THE MAIN TOO HARD ON THE NEW REACH.

STEP 4 SWAP YOUR TILLER AND MAINSHEET HANDS, AND SETTLE DOWN ON YOUR NEW COURSE.

Mastering the gybe

When sailing further off the wind, however, you will quickly tire of going around 'the slow way'.

As with tacking, make a few basic preparations before gybing. Tell the crew of your intentions, saying 'ready to gybe' or 'prepare to gybe'. Check that the water into which you are gybing is clear of obstructions. Work out the course you want to be steering when you come out of the gybe. Lower the centreboard for stability (see page 28). If the wind is gusty, time your gybe so that you gybe in a lull, so there is less chance of being overpowered on the new reach. However, try to gybe when the boat is moving reasonably quickly, as there will be less load on the sails. Watch the wave pattern, and gybe in smooth waters.

When you are ready to gybe, pull the tiller towards you. You need the bow to bear away, coming further off the wind until you are at 180° to the wind direction and then beyond it, onto the opposite gybe. As with tacking, this movement does not have to be dramatic, but you do need to keep up momentum in the turn — it will be quicker than a tack, and you need to ensure that the main comes across cleanly.

The wind direction will move across the stern until it reaches the edge of the mainsail, which will then flick across. Control the movement of the boom by holding the mainsheet between the block on the boom and the block on the deck, and slow it down as it comes across. Keep your body weight as centred as possible.

If you have been on a very broad reach, and it is not too windy, bring the mainsail in slightly before you gybe, so that it does not have to swing through too wide an angle. But make sure that you do not sheet on too hard and too quickly, or the dinghy will be overpowered, heel over and may capsize to leeward.

Once the boom is across, step over and sit on the new windward side, centring the tiller. Work out your new course, and adjust the sails accordingly. You're away on the new gybe!

This process seems straightforward — and it is — but because of the forces involved and the swiftness of the movement, it may take some time to master in windier conditions.

Broaching

Broaching occurs when a gust of wind causes the dinghy to over-power when reaching, and it is blown over. The helmsman loses steerage as the rudder lifts out of the water when the dinghy heels, and the bow rounds up. If the end of the boom hits the water, the boat will capsize to leeward. Keep the boat flat while reaching by easing the main and bearing away when, or slightly before, a gust hits. (On a two-handed boat, the crew should keep an eye out for changes in wind speed.)

You can also broach after coming out of a gybe, if the vang and centreboard are not in the right positions (see The appendages on page 28). Especially when you are racing, boats often tend to wipe out at the gybe or wing mark, when the force of the gybe causes the boat to broach on the new leeward side.

THE DINGHY CAN BROACH — OVERBALANCE AND HEEL HARD TO LEEWARD — WHEN GUSTS HIT. WATCH FOR PUFFS AND EASE THE SHEETS ACCORDINGLY.

Rolling

Sometimes, the dinghy will develop a rocking action around its centre-line when running flat-off. This is known as 'rolling', and there are several ways to minimize this:

■ trim the main more tightly;

■ pull on some more vang to tighten the leech of the main;

■ use the weight of the skipper and crew sitting on opposite sides of the boat to counter the movement;

■ steer in the direction of the rolls, coming up slightly as the dinghy rolls to windward and back down as it rolls to leeward. This keeps the boat under the sails, and should minimize the rolling motion.

WHEN SAILING FLAT-OFF, THE DINGHY MAY DEVELOP A ROLLING MOTION, WHICH COULD THEN RESULT IN A CAPSIZE.

THIS HIGH-PERFORMANCE DINGHY FLIES AN ASYMMETRICAL GENNAKER DOWNWIND, WITH A FIXED TACK.

The spinnaker or gennaker

Many of the two-handed dinghies carry an extra down-wind sail for speed and performance. This lightweight sail is cut round and full to catch as much breeze as possible when sailing downwind. This is called a spin-naker or, more colloquially, the bag, kite or 'chute (as it is made from parachute-like material). This symmet-rical sail is flown forward of the mast on its own small boom, called a spinnaker pole or spinnaker boom, which clips onto the mast and holds out one corner of the sail. Because the spinnaker gets a lot of its power from the wind pushing against it, it can only be hoist-ed when the wind direction is sufficiently far aft. The sail will not be efficient until you are on an angle where its shape can harness the wind.

Many of the modern classes, especially the higher-performance dinghies, have a gennaker, an asymmet-ric downwind sail, which is a cross between a jib and a spinnaker. It is flown in a similar way to a spinnaker, but usually off a fixed pole or bowsprit at the front of the dinghy.

Like other sails, the spinnaker has a head — the top corner of the sail to which the halyard is attached — but instead of having a tack and a clew like a mainsail or jib, it has two clews. This is because the sail is sym-metrical. The corner that is fixed to the spinnaker pole,

and the corner that is free-flying, are alternated as you sail downwind on different gybes. When you are on star-board gybe, the starboard lower corner of the sail will be fixed in position by the spinnaker pole, and the port lower corner will be flying free, attached to the sheet (like the clew of the jib). When you gybe onto port, the pole is brought across and attached to the port sheet. This corner of the sail becomes the fixed point (tack) and the other corner becomes the clew, which is then sheeted. On boats with gennakers, because the sail is asymmetric, the tack is fixed and the sail is gybed like a jib, with the clew passing across the boat.

Many boats have a continuous spinnaker sheet that attaches to one corner of the sail, comes back into the cockpit through blocks, and then runs forward to attach to the other corner of the spinnaker. Some boats have a separate sheet for each side. Either way, the portion of the sheet running aft from the corner of the sail in the spinnaker pole is called the brace or guy, and controls the fore and aft angle of the pole. The portion attached to the sail's free-flowing corner is the sheet. Likewise, a gennaker may also have a continuous sheet. Both ends are tied to the one clew of the sail, while the tack is fixed to the prod at the front of the boat by a tackline. There is no brace or guy on a boat with a gennaker as there is no spinnaker pole.

Spinnaker basics

Every type of dinghy has a slightly different spinnaker system, but the basics remain the same. The sheet and guy will usually run through a pair of blocks, one on each side, attached to the deck on pieces of rope running through a cleat. Attached to the pole is a topping lift or uphaul, running from the top side of the pole to the mast, and a downhaul, running from its underside back onto the deck. These are used to adjust the vertical angle of the pole, making sure that it does not point up too high, or drop too low. On a boat that has a gennaker and a fixed bowsprit or prod, none of these are required.

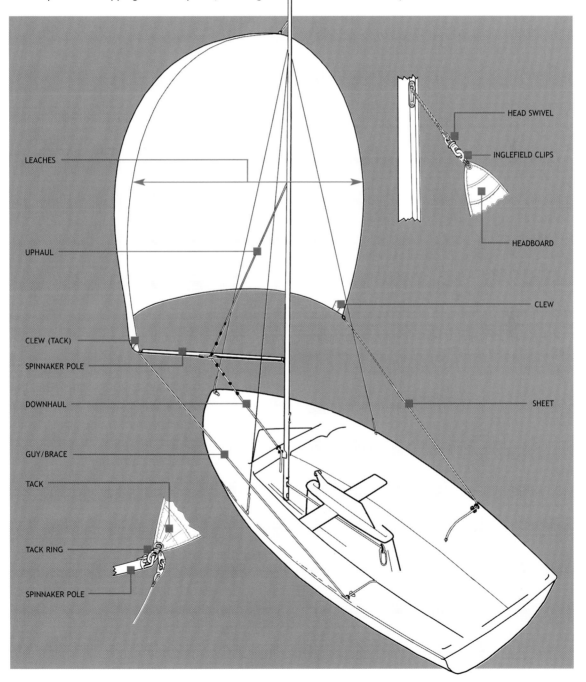

LEACHES

UPHAUL

CLEW (TACK)

SPINNAKER POLE

DOWNHAUL

GUY/BRACE

TACK

TACK RING

SPINNAKER POLE

HEAD SWIVEL

INGLEFIELD CLIPS

HEADBOARD

CLEW

SHEET

Packing the spinnaker

It is important that the spinnaker is not twisted or tangled when it is being hoisted. Before going out on the water, pack the spinnaker carefully into the bag from which it will be launched.

Find the head of the sail, and place it on the ground, pointing away from you. Run your hands along one of the leeches, laying the sail out neatly on the ground until you reach the clew. Work your hands along the other leech, to the second clew. If neither of these sides is twisted, the third side (the foot) will be fine.

Put the foot of the sail into the bag, leaving the clews hanging out the sides. Loosely fold the rest of the sail into the bag — making sure not to re-twist or tangle it — and finish with the head.

Place the spinnaker bag in the boat and attach the halyard to the head of the sail, and the sheets to the clews. It is easier to hoist the spinnaker to leeward (the side further from the wind), because the spinnaker's bulk is blanketed by the mainsail as you hoist it. A gennaker is packed in the same fashion, although as the sail is not symmetrical like a spinnaker, you must separate the head, tack and clew. Tie the halyard to the head of the sail and both sheets to the clew.

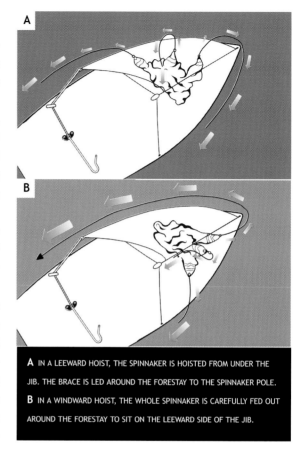

A IN A LEEWARD HOIST, THE SPINNAKER IS HOISTED FROM UNDER THE JIB. THE BRACE IS LED AROUND THE FORESTAY TO THE SPINNAKER POLE.

B IN A WINDWARD HOIST, THE WHOLE SPINNAKER IS CAREFULLY FED OUT AROUND THE FORESTAY TO SIT ON THE LEEWARD SIDE OF THE JIB.

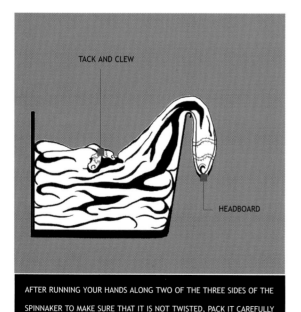

TACK AND CLEW

HEADBOARD

AFTER RUNNING YOUR HANDS ALONG TWO OF THE THREE SIDES OF THE SPINNAKER TO MAKE SURE THAT IT IS NOT TWISTED, PACK IT CAREFULLY INTO ITS BAG, FOOT FIRST.

When you are not racing and if you are sailing in fairly open water, you should be able to gybe onto the appropriate side of the boat to hoist to leeward. While learning to sail, you might want to set up the kite on the port side of the boat, so you can launch and retrieve it while on starboard gybe, which will give you priority, or right of way, if you are sailing near other boats.

The spinnaker sheet running down the dinghy's windward side will be the guy, running through the end of the spinnaker pole. The sheet you use to trim the sail will run down the leeward side.

In a leeward hoist, the spinnaker will be packed and stowed on the leeward side of the dinghy, with the guy, or brace, leading out of the bag, across the foredeck and around the forestay, before leading back through the windward barberhauler and into the cockpit. The sheet will make a much shorter journey, leading around the shrouds and then back through the leeward block into the cockpit of the boat.

Preparing to hoist

The further off the wind you sail, the easier it is to hoist and drop the spinnaker. The boat will sail much flatter, and it will be easier to manipulate the spinnaker pole. While learning, sail flat-off when hoisting and dropping, then come back up on a tighter reach once the spinnaker has been hoisted and set (filled with breeze and trimmed on).

The crew attaches the spinnaker pole to both mast and guy. Pick up the pole off the deck, with the topping lift running upwards and the downhaul down. Feed the brace through the hook at the outboard end of the pole, and clip the inboard end onto the ring on the mast. The pole will probably flop forward.

Adjust the topping lift and outhaul so they are firm, but not so tight that the pole cannot be moved fore and aft. Set the pole's height at about 90° to the mast.

While steering with the tiller between his or her legs, the skipper pulls the halyard to raise the spinnaker to the top of the mast. The crew pulls on the guy to haul the spinnaker's windward clew around to the dinghy's windward side. The corner of the sail should come around and sit at the hook at the outboard end of the pole. The crew cleats off the guy, keeping it in position, and trims the spinnaker with the leeward sheet.

If you are hoisting to windward, the guy is cleated off first; then the sail is fed out of its bag and hauled carefully around to the leeward side, using the sheet.

On a leeward hoist, you can hoist the spinnaker first and then clip on the pole. The skipper pulls up the halyard, and the crew picks up the pole, clips the outboard end onto the guy, pokes it out to windward, and clips the butt of the pole onto the mast. This process is much easier if the yacht has a gennaker.

STEP 1 FEED THE GUY INTO THE OUTBOARD END OF THE POLE AND THEN PUSH IT OUT.

STEP 2 CLIP THE INBOARD END OF THE POLE TO THE MAST, AND ADJUST THE HEIGHT OF THE POLE WITH THE TOPPING LIFT AND DOWNHAUL.

STEP 3 THE SKIPPER PULLS THE HAYARD TO RAISE THE SPINNAKER, WHILE THE CREW PULLS ON THE GUY ON THE WINDWARD SIDE.

STEP 4 MAKE SURE THAT THE SPINNAKER IS FULLY HOISTED, AND ITS CLEW IS IN THE END OF THE POLE.

ONCE THE SPINNAKER HAS BEEN HOISTED AND THE POLE HAS BEEN ADJUSTED, THE SKIPPER CAN HAND OVER THE TRIMMING OF THE SAIL TO THE CREW.

Trimming the spinnaker or gennaker

The spinnaker or gennaker should be sheeted until it is catching the wind efficiently. If the sail is sheeted too loosely, the windward leach will sag and collapse; if it is sheeted too hard, the wind will spill out of it. Keep your eyes on the sail at all times while you are trimming. It is highly responsive, and needs careful attention, especially in fluctuating breezes.

The basic rule is to sheet the spinnaker or gennaker until it fills, then slowly ease it out again until the windward edge starts to curl (which you will see if you are sitting to windward). If you ease it too much, the sail will begin to collapse, so sheet it back on until it sets, then start easing again. The slight curl in the luff is a sign that air is flowing smoothly over the sail, providing the most power. By adjusting the sheet, you are controlling the free-flying corner of the sail, and the adjustments you make will affect the shape of the sail. Due to the shape of the gennaker, it will fly smoothly only at certain wind angles, from around 70 to 110 degrees apparent.

The spinnaker pole should be set as close as possible to 90° to the wind direction so that the maximum sail area is exposed to it. If you are sailing dead downwind, it will be at 90° to the dinghy's centreline. When on a beam reach, the pole should be eased forward so that it is almost touching the forestay. Keep an eye on the wind indicator and set the pole accordingly.

You may be able to adjust the topping lift and downhaul to raise or lower the pole. The clews of the spinnaker should be at the same height. If the breeze is reasonably light, it will hold the spinnaker quite straight out in front, so the pole will be at right angles to the mast. In stronger breezes, it may tend to lift a little higher; raise the end of the pole so that it is at a similar height to the free-flying clew.

Try to ease as soon as the gust hits or, if you can see that a stronger breeze is approaching, ease slightly before it — or you risk being over-powered and may broach. When the wind lightens, you will feel less weight on the sheet and can bring the sail back on again.

As the breeze shifts, the spinnaker and pole need to be trimmed accordingly. Alternatively, the sail can be held in one position and the skipper can steer to the kite; change course slightly to keep the spinnaker full.

If the wind moves forward, move the pole forward so that it is still at right angles to the wind. If the wind moves aft, move it back accordingly.

Hike out to keep the boat flat; ease out the mainsail and spinnaker or gennaker when over-powered in gusts, and bear away in the gusts and steer up in light breezes. If in difficulty, ease the sheet right out to spill wind out of the sail — but never release the guy.

Gybing the spinnaker or gennaker

While you are learning, it may be easier to drop the spinnaker or gennaker before gybing the main, and then re-hoist it on the other side. Before attempting to gybe the spinnaker, you need to master a regular gybe, and be able to steer downwind while trimming the spinnaker or gennaker at the same time.

When sailing a boat with a spinnaker, make sure you are running as flat as possible before attempting a gybe. This way, there will be a minimum of pressure in the spinnaker, so it will be easy for the crew to take the spinnaker pole across. You should then be able to gybe from run to run, on a flat and safe angle.

It is the skipper's job to also keep the spinnaker flying while the crew brings the pole across from one side to the other. If it is trimmed correctly, it should stay full without the pole attached. The skipper has to hold onto both the sheet and the guy to control the sail, but if he is sailing flat, the action of gybing shouldn't upset the spinnaker much. After you have completed the gybe, unclip the butt end of the pole from the mast. Bring in the barber-hauler on this new windward side and pass the pole across the boat in front of the mast. Clip the old sheet — now the guy — to the new outboard end of the pole.

Push the pole out to the corner of the spinnaker, and clip its butt onto the mast. Then adjust the pole according to the direction of the wind. The crew takes the new sheet and starts trimming again.

To gybe a boat with a gennaker, the skipper bears away from the reach to flat-off, then gybes as normal, pulling the helm towards himself and pulling the mainsail over. As there is no spinnaker pole, all the crew have to do is let the old gennaker sheet go and pull hard on the new one, to the clew is pulled around to the other side of the boat.

STEP 1 STEERING WITH THE TILLER BETWEEN HIS KNEES, THE SKIPPER TAKES HOLD OF THE SPINNAKER SHEET AND GUY AND GYBES THE BOAT AS NORMAL. THE MAIN COMES ACROSS, AND THE SKIPPER TRIES TO KEEP THE SPINNAKER FULL.

STEP 2 THE CREW BRINGS THE SPINNAKER POLE ACROSS IN FRONT OF THE MAST, SWAPPING IT END-FOR-END.

STEP 3 THE CREW TAKES CONTROL OF THE SHEET AND GUY, AND TRIMS THE SAIL BACK ON.

STEP 1 THE CREW UNCLIPS THE SPINNAKER POLE FROM THE MAST AND THEN STOWS IT.

STEP 2 EASING THE SPINNAKER SHEET, THE CREW GATHERS IN THE FOOT OF THE SPINNAKER FROM THE WINDWARD SIDE.

STEP 3 THE HALYARD IS RELEASED AND THE BULK OF THE SAIL IS STASHED BACK IN ITS BAG.

STEP 4 THE CREW PACKS AWAY THE HEAD OF THE SAIL AND MAKES SURE THE SHEETS AND HALYARD ARE NOT TWISTED AROUND OTHER LINES.

ALTHOUGH HANDLING THE GENNAKER MAY DEMAND SOME SKILL ON THE PART OF THE SAILOR, MASTERING THIS SKILL WILL PREVENT MISHAPS AND ADD ENORMOUSLY TO THE ENJOYMENT OF THE SAILING EXPERIENCE.

Dropping the spinnaker or gennaker

Although it is easier to hoist to leeward, on a dinghy it is easier to drop the spinnaker or gennaker to windward. If you have stayed on the same gybe since hoisting, or if you have gybed twice, you will be dropping the spinnaker or gennaker on the opposite side to that on which you hoisted it. But if you are now on the opposite gybe, you will be bringing it down on the same side as you hoisted.

Once you have decided to drop the spinnaker or gennaker, make sure the sheets, halyard and tackline are clear to run, without any knots or tangles around objects in the bottom of the boat.

When dropping a spinnaker, the crew unclips the pole off the mast and the guy. Ease the spinnaker sheet and pull on the guy to gather in the foot of the sail on the windward side. Once you have a good grip, release the halyard and stuff the sail back into its bag.

Some boats have a retrieval cord, which pulls the centre of the spinnaker or gennaker back into a sock or chute. If you put the sail away carefully, it shouldn't twist and should be ready for the next hoist.

When dropping a gennaker, the crew grabs the windward sheet and pulls the foot of the sail around to the windward side of the boat. Only once the crew has the foot of the gennaker under control can the halyard be released.

Leeward drops in light weather

On larger boats, the spinnaker is usually dropped to leeward, but this means that the crew would have to move his or her weight to leeward, which would upset the weight balance on a dinghy and cause it to heel. However, you may be able to drop to leeward in light weather. With the crew positioned to leeward, the guy is let go. Gather in the foot of the sail as before, then release the halyard and bring in the body of the sail.

Conquering the Elements

Sailing is often considered complicated and technical because it is at the mercy of unseen — and, to the uninitiated, inexplicable — factors such as wind and water. Sailors have to take into account the unpredictability of weather patterns, and also the risks to safety that may come into play.

Wind, waves and weather

The wind is, by its very nature, invisible, but that does not mean that it cannot be 'seen' — you simply have to know what to look for (see page 48). And while it may seem to be a random force, it can — to a certain extent — be predicted, forecast and analyzed.

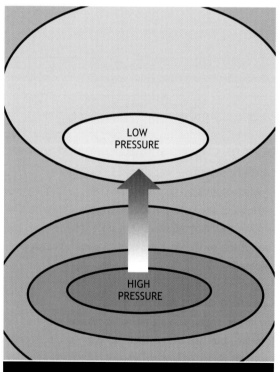

above AIR FLOWS FROM AREAS OF HIGH PRESSURE TO AREAS OF LOW PRESSURE TO CREATE AN EQUILIBRIUM. THIS CREATES WIND.

opposite SAILORS NEED TO UNDERSTAND THE WEATHER AND TIDES IN ORDER TO MAXIMIZE THEIR ENJOYMENT OF THE SPORT.

In the air

Wind is caused by the movement of air between areas of different pressures. Air pressure occurs as a result of gravity, and even on the calmest day the air is in constant, dynamic circulation. Air movement follows the law of physics that all flowing substances (including air) that are subjected to gravity will move until pressure is uniform. Air constantly moves from areas of high pressure towards areas of low pressure in an attempt to form a pressure equilibrium. A difference in air pressure between two places is called a pressure gradient. The greater the gradient — that is, the larger the difference in air pressure in the two places — the stronger the wind, as air flows from high to low pressure.

Because the earth's atmosphere is so vast, air pressure is seldom uniform over a wide area. These differences in pressure are caused by the unequal heating of the earth's surface, and are therefore greatly affected by geographical location — proximity to the sea, a small lake, a large cold lake, a built-up urban area.

When air is heated by both the sun and the land below it, it becomes less dense and expands, causing it to rise. Cooler air flows in to fill the space left by the rising mass of hot air. This movement causes the wind.

Understanding air pressure

Air pressure is measured with a barometer, and expressed in millibars. On a weather map, lines called isobars are drawn to join areas of the same pressure. Wind flows roughly parallel to isobars. In the northern hemisphere, it flows in an anticlockwise direction in low-pressure systems and clockwise in high-pressure systems. The opposite is true in the southern hemisphere. A weather map thus shows the direction in which the wind will blow. How close the isobars are together will show how strong the wind will be.

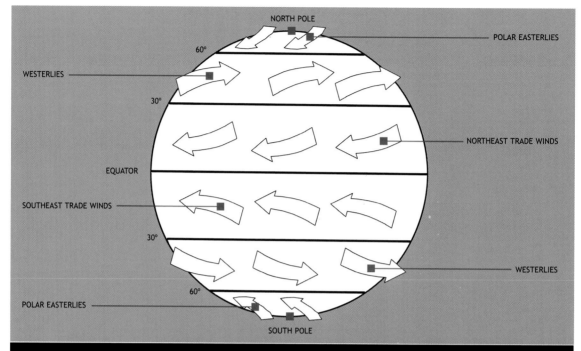

SURFACE WINDS AROUND THE GLOBE FOLLOW A BASIC PATTERN, WHICH IS THEN ALTERED BY LAND AND OCEAN MASSES. ON EACH SIDE OF THE BAND OF LIGHT WINDS NEAR THE EQUATOR ARE THE TRADEWIND ZONES (NORTHEAST IN THE NORTHERN HEMISPHERE AND SOUTHEAST IN THE SOUTHERN HEMISPHERE). BEYOND THESE IS A BAND OF PREDOMINANTLY WESTERLY WINDS, IN THE TEMPERATE LATTITUDES.

Surface winds

While wind and weather conditions are always intensely local and are affected by many different factors, the earth is roughly divided into a series of pressure zones.

Immediately above and below the equator is a band characterized largely by very light winds. This zone, called the doldrums, or the horse latitudes, was the bane of trading and transport sailing ships, and still frequently causes frustration to round-the-world yachtsmen. On either side of the doldrums are the trade wind latitudes, where the wind blows predominantly northeast (in the northern hemisphere) or southeast (in the southern hemisphere). Above and below these latitudes is a band of predominant westerlies. This zone, between 30° and 60° latitude, experiences changeable weather, but the wind direction and movement of weather systems is predominantly west to east. Most of the major sailing nations fall within this band of temperate westerlies — the northern United States and the United Kingdom in the northern hemisphere, and South Africa, Australia and New Zealand in the southern hemisphere.

The earth's atmosphere is always in motion. The weather in the temperate latitudes is usually influenced by the movement of depressions (areas of low pressure) and anticyclones (areas of high pressure), in a generally eastward motion. Along with these zones of varying pressure come various types of fronts — borders between air masses usually associated with precipitation (such as rain and snow) and changes in wind direction.

Anticyclones — indicated by an *H* for high pressure on the weather map — are usually associated with fine, settled weather. In the centres of these air masses, the pressure is usually quite uniform, so there is very little pressure gradient and, therefore, little wind.

When your area is being affected by a depression or low-pressure system (indicated by an *L* for low pressure on the weather map), conditions are more likely to be windy, with rain.

One of the most striking examples of how the uneven heating of land and sea can cause wind is the sea breeze, which occurs in many coastal locations. A sea breeze occurs on fine, otherwise settled days with little natural gradient breeze — in periods of uniform high pressure.

The sun beating down from a clear sky warms the land and the air in contact with it. By the middle of the day and the early afternoon, this warm layer of air has expanded, become less dense, and started to rise. This means air pressure is lower over the land than the sea, which is covered by a cooler layer of more dense air.

A pressure gradient is established, so cool air flows from the higher pressure over the sea to the low-pressure area over the land.

Out at sea, air flows downward to replace the cool air that has flowed ashore. This creates a return flow above the sea breeze layer, which completes the cycle. This motion is called the sea breeze circulation, and can cause a rather fresh breeze.

The hotter the day, and the larger the area of land being heated, the stronger the breeze. This breeze will often continue to blow into the early evening, only dying as the land begins to cool down and uniform pressure is restored.

One of the most famous and reliable sea breezes in the world is the Fremantle Doctor, which blows at Fremantle in Western Australia, where the 1987 America's Cup was held. Because of the vast size of the Australian continent and its inland desert, a very strong sea breeze circulation pattern occurs almost every day, creating a fresh, reliable breeze of around 20 knots.

The sea breeze is especially good for learners because it is always onshore. No matter what happens to you while you are out on the water, it will always be easier for you to make your way back to shore — the wind will simply blow you back in!

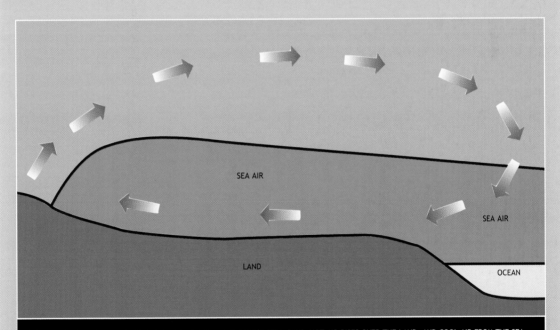

SEA AIR

SEA AIR

LAND

OCEAN

THE SEA BREEZE CIRCULATION IS ESTABLISHED ON FINE, OTHERWISE STILL DAYS. HOT AIR RISES OVER THE LAND, AND COOL AIR FROM THE SEA FLOWS ONSHORE TO REPLACE IT.

Local conditions

Wind conditions will be influenced largely by the local geography of the specific region. Headlands create shelter from certain wind directions. Wind bends around relief features, funnels down valleys, spills down off hills and forms ripples on the surface of the sea. The shape of the coastline, the position of offshore islands, and how exposed to the ocean your sailing location is will have an impact on how each wind direction manifests itself.

Certain wind directions are onshore, offshore and cross-shore. Some wind directions will create waves and swell, others produce calm seas, and some will create a lee shore for launching and retrieval. Some wind directions will also feel colder than others, depending on whether they are blowing from the poles or the tropics, off the sea, or off the land. All these elements will affect local conditions.

Wind direction may also be associated with certain weather patterns: a southerly may bring cold showers and an easterly may only blow during settled weather.

Get to know the area in which you plan to sail. Observe it on different days, in different weather conditions and at times when different wind directions are at play. Talk to other sailors about weather patterns in your area. You will quickly get to know the characteristics of your local conditions. Observe and learn.

Weather forecasts

■ **Newspapers** Most newspapers run a brief forecast. Once you have learnt the basics, you may be able to predict the weather by observing pressure systems, the proximity of fronts, and how close the isobars are. These, combined with a short forecast, will give you an idea of what to expect. However, wind strengths will probably be in kph or mph, rather than knots, and it will not be as detailed as a marine forecast. Also, it will be some 12 hours old.

■ **Television and radio** This is likely to be an indication only, but will be more up-to-date than the newspaper.

■ **Telephone** The meteorological office in your area runs a telephonic weather information service. This will be updated regularly, and will usually have a marine forecast, which will cover wind and wave conditions at sea, and maybe tides. Some regional services may provide readings for wind strengths at local landmarks.

■ **Internet** There are many sources of weather information on the Internet, from weather maps and satellite pictures to written forecasts.

■ **Harbourmasters** Most harbours, yacht clubs and coastguard stations will display the most up-to-date forecasts on noticeboards.

LAKES, ESPECIALLY THOSE SURROUNDED BY HIGH GROUND, MAY EXPERIENCE DISTINCT LOCAL WIND, WEATHER AND WAVE CONDITIONS.

BEAUFORT SCALE

Wind force	Wind speed (knots)	Wind description	Wave height	On the sea	On the land
0	0-1	Calm	0	Flat, mirror-like sea	Smoke creates vertical column
1	1-3	Light air movement	0.1m (⅓ft)	Scale-like ripples, but no crests of foam	Wind direction indicated by smoke, but weather vanes not affected
2	4-6	Light breeze	0.5m (1½ft)	Wavelets, with glass-like crests that do not break	Weather vanes move, leaves rustle
3	7-10	Gentle breeze	1m (3½ft)	Larger wavelets, with crests that begin to break; glassy foam, and occasional white horses	Noticeable movement of leaves and twigs
4	11-16	Moderate breeze	2m (6½ft)	Small waves, with regular white horses	Movement of branches and debris/litter, with some dust
5	17-21	Fresh breeze	3m (10ft)	Moderate waves, which are longer and with many white horses; some spray	Noticeable movement in small trees; inland water has small wavelets with crests
6	22-27	Strong breeze	4m (13ft)	Large waves, with extensive white foam crests; some spray	Noticeable movement of large branches; clear gusts of wind
7	28-33	Near gale	5m (16½ft)	Choppy sea, with white foam crests blown in streaks	Trees sway, and walking upwind is difficult
8	34-40	Gale	6m (19½ft)	Relatively high waves, with crest edges beginning to break into spindrift; foam forms noticeable streaks	Trees lose branches, and walking upwind is very difficult
9	41-47	Strong gale	7m (23ft)	High waves, with clear foam streaks; crests begin to tumble and fall; visibility affected by sea spray	Some damage to structures such as roofs and chimneys
10	48-55	Storm	9m (30ft)	Very high waves, with long, curved crests that result in large areas of white streaks of foam; heavy tumbling; visibility noticeably affected	Whole trees uprooted; considerable structural damage

YOU CAN LEARN TO USE SEA CONDITIONS TO YOUR ADVANTAGE — SUCH AS UTILIZING WAVES IN ORDER TO SURF DOWNWIND.

Tides, currents and waves

If you are sailing on the sea, tides and currents will be a very important factor to consider — and understand. Some areas have only slight tidal streams, while others have enormous differences between high and low tides, creating very strong flows. The tides will influence how, when and where you launch your dinghy — and how far up the beach you should leave your trailer! All but the smallest tides will also have an effect on your sailing, because the movement of water will affect how the dinghy moves, and the wave conditions. In narrow areas and near features such as islands or headlands, the movement of water caused by the rise and fall of the tide may also make it difficult to control your dinghy. You need to be aware of this so that you aren't drawn onto the rocks — or worse, out to sea.

In most places, the tide rises and falls twice a day — two high tides and two low tides. The height of a tide is measured from a base point, called chart datum, set at the level of the lowest possible tide in any particular area. Tide heights are measured at height above chart datum, so a low tide might be 1.1m (3ft 7in) and a high tide 3.5m (11ft 6in, or 11½ft).

The distance between the height of these two tides — that is, between what is commonly known as high and low water — is called the tidal range. When the tidal range is small — for example, a 1.6m (5ft 3in) low and a 2.2m (7ft 3in) high — the movement of water will not be very great, so tidal currents will not be very strong. When the range is large — 1.1m (3ft 7in) to 3.6m (11ft 10in), for example — tidal flows will be quite noticeable. The tidal range exceeds 10m (33ft) in some areas

Following the cycles

Because the tidal cycle takes approximately 12½ hours from high tide to high tide, the time of the high tide moves on by about an hour each day. For example, if the tide is high at 8am, it will be high again at approximately 8.30pm that night, and again around 9am the following day.

Every area has a basic tidal range, which varies over a monthly and yearly cycle of tidal ranges. Extra-high tides and very low ones are generally referred to as spring tides, and occur roughly twice a month, at full and new moon. The height of the tide can also be affected by other factors such as low air pressure and strong onshore winds.

Newspapers, nautical almanacs, yacht club handbooks and some magazines publish daily or monthly tide charts. These will show the times of the high tides in your area, and maybe the lows (if they do not show the lows, they will fall approximately six hours after the highs). They should also show the height of the tide, so you can estimate the tidal range.

The time of the tide varies along the coastline, so you may have to adjust the basic tide time to suit your particular location. Your local paper or almanac may give you a guide — a number of minutes to add or subtract to obtain an accurate tide time for your area.

Again, get to know your local area or ask someone experienced so that you know what to expect. Work out the size of the usual tidal range in the area in which you plan to launch and retrieve, too, so you do not have a long walk back to your trailer after the tide has retreated across the mud flats!

As well as the water flow caused by the rising and falling of the tide, the sea, rivers and some large lakes — especially those into which and from which rivers flow — also experience other currents. As with the wind, water bends around islands, promontories and other geographical features.

Areas where the sea bottom shelves or areas of deeper water produce different water movements. Again, observe, be aware and feel free to ask for advice about your particular area.

The rule of 12

The tide builds up momentum as it runs in and out, and runs strongest in the middle of each cycle.

A useful approximation is the rule of 12: in the first hour of the tide rising or falling, only $1/12$ of the total volume of water will move in or out. In the second hour, it is $2/12$ (or $1/6$); then in the third and fourth hours, $3/12$ ($1/4$) in each hour.

This means that in the middle two hours of the tidal cycle, $6/12$, or half, the water flow occurs. This is usually when the tide is running at its strongest, and will have its greatest effect. In the fifth hour, the flow drops back to $2/12$ ($1/6$), then back to the final $1/12$ in the last hour.

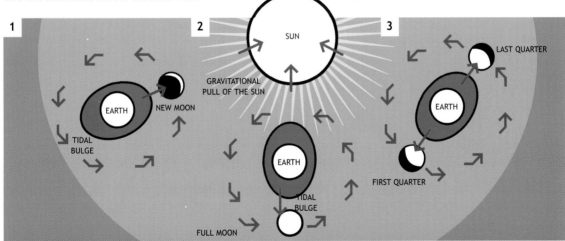

1 NEW MOON WITH THE SUN AND MOON ALIGNED, THEIR COMBINED GRAVITATIONAL PULL CREATES THE HIGHEST SPRING TIDES (MAXIMUM DIFFERENCE BETWEEN HIGH AND LOW WATER).

2 FULL MOON ALTHOUGH THE SUN AND THE MOON ARE IN LINE, THEIR GRAVITATIONAL PULL IS IN OPPOSITION; BUT THIS ALSO RESULTS IN SPRING TIDES.

3 FIRST AND LAST QUARTERS OF THE MOON THE SUN AND THE MOON ARE NOT ALIGNED; THIS PRODUCES NEAP TIDES, THOSE WITH LEAST VARIATION BETWEEN HIGH AND LOW TIDES.

Safety at sea

Knowing what the weather is likely to do is your first safeguard against being caught out in adverse conditions. While you are still learning to sail, it is probably better to err on the side of caution: if you don't like the look of the weather, don't go sailing. Build up your confidence and practise your skills in ideal conditions before you tackle challenges that will test your competence. Always remember that you cannot control the wind and sea; you can harness their power and learn to make the best of them, but you cannot stop them from turning nasty.

Beyond the basics of reading a weather forecast (see also Weather forecasts on page 74) and telling someone where you are going and when to expect you back, there are other steps you can take to ensure your sailing experiences are safe and positive. The key to safe sailing is to retain respect for the wind and water, being prepared, having the right equipment and generally using your common sense.

Boat and skipper licensing

Even in advanced sailing countries, it may not be necessary for a dinghy to be registered, or its skipper licensed. Yachting New Zealand, for example, holds a register of keelboats and their owners and issues sail numbers, but this does not apply to dinghies. It is, therefore, safest to check with your local authorities before buying a dinghy or taking one out on the water.

Likewise, insurance may not be mandatory – but is advisable. Insure the boat for the area in which you will sail, and how you intend to use it (racing insurance will generally be more expensive). Make sure that your trailer is also insured, and that the dinghy is insured while being transported as well as on the water.

Many sailing organizations and clubs offer boat safety courses for volunteers, and these will help you become a safe sailor. These classes cover the basics of safety, boat handling and navigation for the novice and experienced sailor, and some may even include proficiency courses specially designed for dinghy sailors.

KNOWING YOUR OWN LIMITS IS ONE OF THE KEYS TO ENJOYING YOUR SAILING EXPERIENCE.

IN MANY COUNTRIES, BOAT LICENSING OR REGISTRATION ARE MANDATORY FOR LARGE YACHTS, BUT NOT DINGHIES.

Basic safety equipment should be carried on board at all times when sailing. Many dinghies have storage bags attached to the sides of the cockpit, or lockers where small items can be safely stowed.

■ **Lifejackets** Lifejackets and buoyancy aids are always essential.

■ **Rope** Carry a line or rope suitable for towing. The mainsheet on some dinghies may be suitable.

■ **Pump** Some dinghies may have built-in drainage, but to be safe carry a small pump or alternative means of bailing the cockpit, such as a bucket or scoop and/or a sponge.

■ **Signals** If you do get into difficulties, the easiest way to show you need help is by raising and lowering your arms repeatedly, but you can also make yourself more visible with brightly coloured fabric or a mirror. Most dinghies do not provide adequate dry storage for hand-held flares or small smoke signals, but if you have a suitable place for these, then carry them, but take special note of their expiry date.

■ **Repair tape** Waterproof tape and/or sailmakers' sticky-back tape may also be handy for repairs on the water.

■ **Anchor** In many small racing dinghies it may be impractical to carry an anchor and warp, but if your boat is large enough, these may prove invaluable.

■ **Protection** Protect your body against the elements by carrying sunscreen and drinking water.

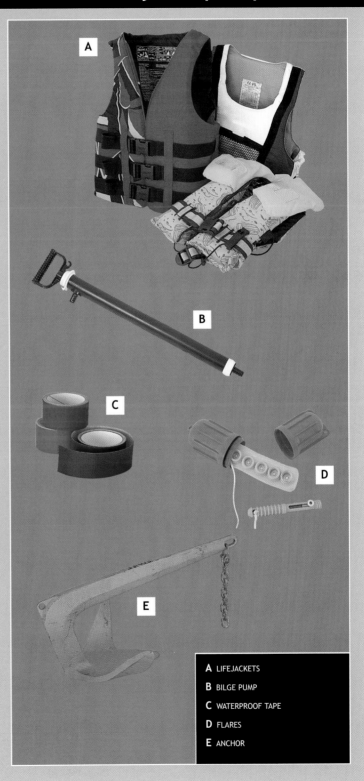

A LIFEJACKETS

B BILGE PUMP

C WATERPROOF TAPE

D FLARES

E ANCHOR

Sailing clothes

Clothing is an important part of your safety equipment. The right clothing will keep you warm and dry, offer some buoyancy, and will protect you from sunburn. Even on a fine day, the breeze and the lower surface temperature of the water will mean that it is cooler out on the water than on land. If you are wet — even a few splashes — the wind chill factor will increase, so it is better to wear too much gear and take some off if necessary than spoil your sail by feeling cold and miserable.

Outer gear

In tropical areas and at the height of summer in temperate zones, the air temperature may be warm enough to sail in shorts and a T-shirt, but remember that all exposed flesh will be susceptible to sunburn. Wear a lightweight wind-breaker jacket or long-sleeved cotton top to keep off the sun.

Headgear

A hat, either the peaked type or the more nautical style with a rim all round, will be handy. Tie or clip one end of a length of string or elastic cord to the back of the hat, and the other to your jacket collar or T-shirt label, so even if the hat is lifted off by the wind, it will stay attached to you.

Wetsuits

For cooler days or wave conditions where you are likely to get quite wet, a wetsuit may be a better option. The stretchy neoprene fabric will trap water in a layer over your skin, where it is warmed by your body and acts as insulation against the cold.

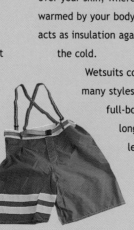

Wetsuits come in many styles, from the full-body type with long sleeves and leggings that are usually worn by surfers and divers, to the 'shorties' often worn by waterskiers, which have short legs and sleeves, or no sleeves at all.

The most practical style for sailing is probably long-legged wetsuits (added protection for your knees) without sleeves, so your arms are free to move.

Wetsuit fabric also comes in different thicknesses, offering varying levels of insulation against the cold. Choose a suitable thickness for the temperatures in which you are likely to be sailing.

The wetsuit should be tight enough to sit close to your skin without being baggy, but not so tight that it restricts movement.

Wear your underwear or your bathing suit underneath, but the more the wetsuit touches your skin, the more efficient the insulating property of the water layer. Wear a T-shirt and shorts to protect your shoulders and arms from sunburn and the backside of the wetsuit from excessive wear on the textured surface of the deck.

Drysuits

Drysuits are a more expensive option, and are worn by many competitive sailors. They are designed to keep all water away from the skin, and completely enclose the body from wrists to ankles. They are made of two layers of waterproof fabric with a layer of rubber sandwiched between them, with rubber seals at the neck, wrists and ankles, or built-in booties. These suits do not offer quite the same insulation properties as the wetsuits, so it may be a good idea to wear a layer of warm clothing underneath your drysuit.

Waterproof gear

Keelboat sailors frequently wear custom-made wet-weather gear, consisting of bibbed trousers and a raincoat-style jacket, made of weatherproof material. While this type of clothing is practical in a situation where you are sitting on the side of a large boat getting the occasional splash, it is impractical for dinghy sailing. If you capsize or fall into the water, it will quickly become waterlogged and drag you under. Also, general wet-weather gear can be too bulky and restrict your movements.

Lightweight bibbed trousers in a waterproof fabric — worn perhaps over a T-shirt or long-sleeved, light cotton shirt — will, on the other hand, be suitable for dinghy sailing.

Wool garments stay warm even when wet, but the best option are tops and leggings made from polypropylene, a synthetic material. These are lightweight and thin so can be worn under other clothing, and they have excellent thermal properties and dry quite rapidly.

Footwear

Although it may be comfortable to sail with bare feet, it is safer and more practical to wear light shoes with grip soles — like other sailing gear, available from sports shops and chandleries — or wetsuit boots. These will help keep your feet dry and warm, as well as offer extra grip on the cockpit floor and preventing you from stubbing your toes on blocks or the centreboard.

Gloves

You might find it easier to wear gloves to protect your hands and give you a better grip on the sheets. Chandlery shops sell leather gloves with cut-off fingertips specifically designed for sailing. These will give you the grip you need and, because they tend to last for a long time, may well be worth the investment.

Staying afloat

There are many kinds of simple buoyancy aids or life-jackets. In most the buoyancy is provided by closed-cell foam. They range from the lightweight, close-fitting buoyancy vests to full lifejackets with behind-the-head buoyancy designed to support an unconscious person in a face-up position in the water. A full lifejacket is probably more of a hindrance than a help in dinghy sailing. The new inflatable models are much less bulky, but they are more suitable for keelboat sailing, where you are unlikely to fall into the water and need to deploy the jacket. When dinghy sailing, you are likely to spend some time in the water, and do not want to frequently have to inflate and deflate a lifejacket.

Buoyancy aids

Your buoyancy aid should not be too bulky, but support your weight when in the water. It needs to be fitted to your body shape so that it doesn't ride up when you are sailing or in the water, preventing you from swimming around to right the boat. Many styles are close-fitting, attached with clips or Velcro straps for a snug fit, which offer suitable buoyancy and added warmth. Talk to your local yacht club, sailing instructor or chandlery about which model will be most suitable for you.

Built-in buoyancy and drainage

Most sailing boats have in-built buoyancy, but they are simply not designed to be sailed while full of water.

Many boats have self-draining cockpits, open at the back so water can flow back out of them. Others have self-bailing systems, called venturis. These slots in the floor can be opened when the boat is sailing downwind, to suck the water out. There is also the conventional method of using a hand-bailer, bucket or sponge.

The dinghy may have a drain hole in the transom, with a plug called a bung. This may help drain the cockpit on land (remove the bung and lift the bow so the water runs out) or to drain the space between the decks and cockpit and the bottom of the hull.

Rules of the road at sea

The International Collision Regulations apply to all craft on the water, sail or power, on salt- or fresh water. Everyone who goes out on the water should know them, and demonstrate a responsible attitude.

But never assume that someone else knows the rules: if they seem to be on a collision course with you, be ready to alter course yourself — even if you are in the right. Admitting afterwards that they should have given way to you won't do any good if both boats are damaged, and people may have been injured. Failure to comply with the rules means you can be prosecuted and fined, and your insurance may not be valid.

Basic rules

■ **Look out** It is the responsibility of every vessel to maintain a look out at all times to avoid collisions. This may be quite straightforward on a sailing dinghy when you are looking around for the breeze anyway, but quite often larger boats may be driven by autopilot, or have blind spots. Keep a good look out yourself, and do not assume that people on other boats have seen you. Don't hesitate to call out to alert them to your presence.

■ **Power gives way to sail** In most situations, a power-driven vessel gives way to a sailing vessel. However, sailboats still have to give way to fishing vessels, vessels they are overtaking (even if it is a power boat) and any vessel restricted in its ability to manoeuvre, for example, dredging or doing other work that means it cannot change course. This means that — most of the time — power-driven vessels such as speedboats and launches will give way to you, but as the stand-on vessel — that is, the boat with priority over the give-way vessel — you have responsibilities too. It is your duty to maintain your course and speed so that the other boat can avoid you. Do not alter course to avoid them unless it is apparent that they are not changing course for you. If this is the case, reduce speed and stop by coming head-to-wind, or turn away from the direction from which the approaching boat is coming.

■ **Common sense** Common sense demands that very small vessels do not impede large vessels, so be sure to keep clear.

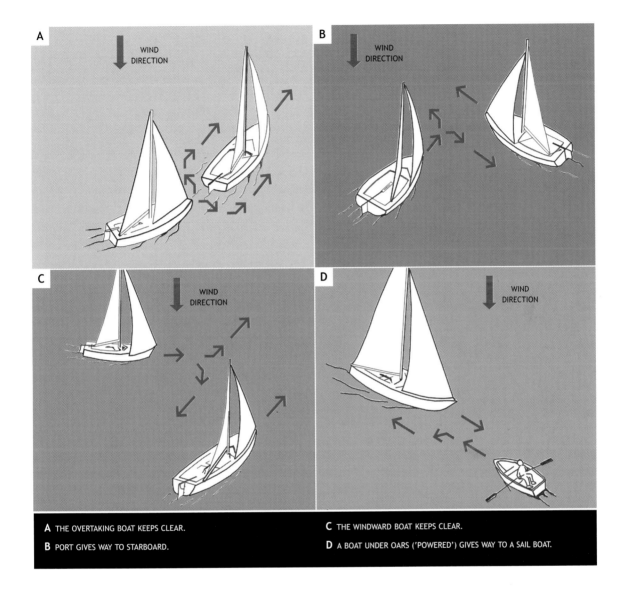

A THE OVERTAKING BOAT KEEPS CLEAR.

B PORT GIVES WAY TO STARBOARD.

C THE WINDWARD BOAT KEEPS CLEAR.

D A BOAT UNDER OARS ('POWERED') GIVES WAY TO A SAIL BOAT.

■ **Port and starboard** Boats that are sailing on starboard tack — that is, with the wind coming over the starboard side, with the boom on the port side — have priority over boats sailing on port tack. This applies if you are sailing upwind or downwind. If both boats are on the same tack, but on converging courses (if one boat is tacking upwind and another is running downwind towards it), the windward boat must keep clear.

If you are on starboard tack, look for boats approaching on port. Call 'Starboard!' to alert them to your priority status — but be prepared to alter course if necessary. To avoid the other boat, turn to starboard, away from the direction it is approaching.

If you are on port tack and see that you are on a collision course with a boat on starboard, you will have two choices: either tack onto starboard yourself, so that you are sailing parallel to them, or alter course to dip behind their stern by bearing away slightly if you are sailing upwind. Make your change of course early — and make sure that it is obvious — so that the other boat knows you have seen it and are going to do something about it!

■ **Overtaking** If you are sailing a performance-oriented dinghy, you may find yourself passing other boats. It is then the responsibility of the overtaking boat to keep clear of the boat it is passing.

THE MOST BASIC OF RULES IS THAT POWER GIVES WAY TO SAIL.

■ **Marked channels, fairways and lanes** When you are sailing in a channel, keep as far to the right-hand side of the channel as possible. When passing another boat in a head-on situation, keep to the right, and allow the other vessel to pass on your port side. Also, small boats should not impede the progress of larger craft in such channels, as their manoeuvrability may be restricted by their draught.

Getting to know your area

If you are learning to sail on your own, rather than at a sailing club or school, it is important that you learn about the area in which you will be sailing. It may also be useful to learn how to read nautical charts, which contain much valuable information: the depth of the water, the tides affecting it, the bottom, the coastline and its features — such as rocks or reefs — and aids to navigation. When dinghy sailing, you will usually not be very far offshore, but chart-reading skills and using a compass will come in handy if you start sailing larger boats, or racing.

Know the signals

Most countries follow a universal system for buoys, beacons and other navigational signals. These are erected mainly for the convenience of commercial shipping, and mark channels and navigational hazards such as sandbanks, rocks and reefs, and submerged objects.

These may not be vital to a dinghy sailor but, as you get to know your local waters, it may be worth learning what they are and what they indicate.

■ **Lateral marks** delineate channels, especially lanes where ships enter and leave a harbour. In most countries, red buoys indicate the port-hand side of the channel coming into a harbour, and green ones show the starboard side (the opposite is true in the USA). The reverse applies when you leave a harbour. In larger harbours, buoys may be numbered. Green marks have odd numbers and red marks even.

■ **Cardinal marks** indicate dangers such as rocks and reefs. They are placed on the extremities of the hazard and indicate in which direction (north, south, east or west of the mark) safe water lies. They have a yellow-and-black striped pole and a pair of triangles on the top that show which side it is safe to pass on.

■ **Isolated danger marks** point out specific hazards, which have clear water all around them, such as rocks. They have black-and-red striped pillars, and two black balls on the top. You can pass on any side of them.

■ **Special marks** are yellow, and can be round, square, cone-shaped or pillars. They indicate a special feature under water: the end of a sewage pipeline, a military exercise zone, or the position of an underwater cable.

IN MOST PLACES, RED MARKS INDICATE THE PORT SIDE OF A CHANNEL WHEN ENTERING A HARBOUR. THESE CAN BE CAN-SHAPED BUOYS OR POLES WITH A SQUARE ON TOP. GREEN MARKS WITH A TRIANGULAR SHAPE INDICATE THE STARBOARD SIDE OF THE CHANNEL.

Dinghy sailing is not a dangerous sport, but there is potential for minor injuries and conditions caused by exposure to the elements.

■ **Cuts and bruises** On windy days, and in the cut and thrust of dinghy racing, there is always the potential for minor cuts and bruising. If you have a dry spot on your boat, carry a small first-aid kit. Wearing the right clothing will also help prevent injuries to feet and hands, and a wetsuit will make kneeling and hiking out more comfortable. Also remember to keep your head clear of the boom while tacking and gybing.

■ **Seasickness** Because of the size of the boat and its motion in the waves, you are unlikely to be seasick when dinghy sailing.

There are medications for seasickness, but these may make you drowsy. An alternative is acupressure wrist bands, which apply pressure to a point on the wrist that is believed to suppress motion sickness.

If you are seasick, drink plenty of water so that you don't become dehydrated — especially important in hot weather. Always carry water on your boat, and drink regularly. Even if it isn't that hot, you will probably be sweating through exertion, and need to top up your bodily fluids.

■ **Sunburn** Sailors are particularly susceptible to sunburn, since light is reflected off the surface of the sea and light-coloured boat decks, as well as coming straight from the sun. Remember to apply plenty of sunscreen to exposed parts of your body, even under your chin and on the underside of your nose. Wear a hat and long-sleeved clothing. See Getting into gear on pages 80–81.

■ **Hypothermia** This condition occurs when the temperature of the body drops. This can be very dangerous, and can even be fatal. Wear adequate clothing to avoid getting cold. If you do become very cold — especially if you have spent some time in the water after a capsize — go ashore and warm up with a hot shower. Eat regularly, go ashore when you start to tire, and at least make an effort to keep dry.

Uncontrollable shivering is the first symptom of lowered body temperature, followed by numbness in the extremities, loss of dexterity and clumsiness. As the condition starts to deteriorate, the shivering may stop, and the victim can also become incoherent and eventually lose consciousness.

In minor cases of hypothermia, prevent the sufferer from getting any colder. The body needs to rewarm itself, so get the victim off the water, into a hot shower or into some dry clothes, and give them a warm, sweet drink (not alcohol). In more severe cases, it is important that you call for proper medical help urgently.

SUNBURN IS A FREQUENT HAZARD FOR SAILORS WHO DO NOT TAKE THE NECESSARY PRECAUTIONS AGAINST THE SUN.

Where to from Here?

above and opposite ONCE HAVING MASTERED THE BASIC SAILING SKILLS, ARDENT SAILORS MAY PROGRESS FURTHER, LEADING TO CLOSE AND EXHILIRATING RACING IN HIGH-PERFORMANCE DINGHIES.

erhaps one of the most exciting and satisfying aspects of dinghy sailing is that, no matter how much you do it or how experienced you become, you can never know everything, or stop improving. Because of the variable nature of wind and water, and frequent advances in boat and sail design and technology, even people who have been sailing all their lives can learn new skills or gain experience in different situations. You never stop learning — and you certainly never stop enjoying yourself.

Unchartered waters

Mastering the basics of dinghy sailing can lead you onto many other aspects of the sport. Someone who has learnt how sailing works, how to set up a boat, steer a course and trim sails will be welcome on almost any yacht. The skills learnt on a 12-foot dinghy will be just as applicable on a 120-foot racing yacht — just on a larger scale, involving bigger loads and greater speed. Learning to sail a dinghy yourself, rather than taking a crew position on a keelboat and only learning one position — or a even a series of tasks — will stand you in much greater stead, and make you a useful, informed and adaptable member of any crew.

Of course, you can learn the basics of sailing in a weekend. However, becoming a competent, confident sailor or crew takes time and experience. So much of sailing is developing the ability to feel when things are right and the boat is trimmed, set up and being sailed correctly. Fortunately, developing this feeling is part of the fun, and is what makes sailing enjoyable and challenging right from the start.

Once you have mastered the basics, however, what are your options? Where can the sport take you? What else is there to do?

International Sailing Federation (ISAF)

The International Sailing Federation is the worldwide governing authority for sailing. It has 121 member nations and manages the sailing events at the Olympic Games, as well as developing and administrating the International Yacht Racing Rules and Regulations. There are 87 ISAF International, Recognised and Classic Yacht classes worldwide, from the little Optimist Dinghy to the largest the 60 foot racing multihull class. Find out more at www.sailing.org

Dinghy racing

You need to be confident of your basic sailing, manoeuvring and trimming skills before venturing onto the race course. However, racing adds an extremely exciting, challenging and satisfying dimension to the recreational sport. It adds a psychological dimension to the physical process of harnessing the wind, requiring a knowledge of certain rules, an understanding of wind shifts and their effects on both the water and your vessel, and a competitive urge.

Racing is not for everybody and, in larger fleets, it is certainly not for the faint-hearted! But, as with the recreational element of dinghy sailing, you will continue to learn because every race is different to another: various competitors, changing wind and water conditions, and even your changing approach and attitude will affect the outcome.

Many sailing schools and clubs running beginners' courses also have programmes for learning and refining racing skills, including group and one-on-one coaching clinics. You will also need to learn the international racing rules, which govern acceptable manoeuvres in various situations. It is very important to know and understand these rules when racing at close quarters.

Be prepared

When buying or borrowing a boat as a novice, you should have considered whether or not you want to race in the future, so hopefully you will have access to a dinghy you can race in your area. Contact your local sailing club and find out when and where they hold races.

Face the fact that you probably won't do very well in the beginning, but remember that everybody started in the same position – from the experienced children racing around you to America's Cup skippers. Everyone has come last at some time in their sailing careers – and it is a sobering fact that it can happen to even the most knowledgeable sailor at any time!

Keeping a sailing diary can be helpful. Record the details of each race in which you compete: the date, time, wind and weather conditions, what happened during the race, what you felt you learnt, what went well, what went wrong, aspects on which you feel you can improve. If you can, talk about your experiences with a sailing friend or coach. And don't forget in the heat of the moment that sailing is supposed to be fun.

ONE-DESIGN CLASSES, SUCH AS THE LASER, OFFER CLOSE, EXCITING RACING BECAUSE THE BOATS ARE SO EVENLY MATCHED, PLACING THE EMPHASIS ON THE SKILLS OF THE SKIPPER.

THE TEMPERATE CLIMES AND SHELTERED WATERS OF ILLE AUX CERFS IN MAURITIUS OFFER IDEAL OPPORTUNITIES FOR THE HOLIDAYMAKER TO VENTURE OUT INTO THE WATER FOR THE FIRST TIME, ALLOWING FOR A MEMORABLE SAILING EXPERIENCE.

Sailing in exotic locations

Many international resorts run sailing programmes and these may be your best chance to sail in ideal conditions: fine weather, flat water, and moderate, constant breeze.

The Mediterranean

Numerous resorts on the Mediterranean coast offer sailing tuition or the use of boats as an optional extra or part of a holiday package. Some areas may be crowded and the water a little polluted to qualify as a sailing haven, but you can certainly experience great conditions on the coasts of Spain, France, Italy, Croatia, Greece and into Turkey.

The Caribbean

A very popular destination for holidaymakers from the USA, the islands of the Caribbean have offered some of the most sought-after sailing waters in the world since the times of the Spanish Main. Once again, many resorts offer sailing schools and courses. The waters surrounding most of the Caribbean islands have the turquoise shade created by coral sand and the area is blessed with steady, warm northeast trade winds from the Atlantic.

The Indian Ocean islands

The crystal-clear waters and warm weather of the Maldives and Mauritius in the Indian Ocean offer a dream location for sailing. The Maldivian archipelago has resorts scattered across its small, low-lying coral islands, while the 330km (205 miles) coastline of Mauritius is almost entirely surrounded by one of the world's largest unbroken coral reefs, making for sheltered, idyllic sailing conditions.

The islands of the Pacific

There are literally thousands of islands in the vast Pacific Ocean, many of which are popular tourist destinations. These, too, provide warm conditions, trade winds and sheltered waters inside tropical coral lagoons. Popular destinations include the French Polynesian islands of New Caledonia and Tahiti. The tropical zone of northern Queensland, Australia also has the advantages of regular trade winds, warm waters and coral reefs.

Further south in the temperate zone, the spectacular harbours of Sydney, Australia (host to the 2000 Olympic regatta) and Auckland, New Zealand (hosted the America's Cup in 2000 and 2003) offer a less tropical but equally exciting sailing experience.

Crewing for others

Even if you want to sail single-handed or be the helms-man of a double-handed dinghy, crewing for an experi-enced sailor on a two-handed boat can be an excellent way to develop your skills and learn from someone who knows more than you can ever glean from a book. This is especially true when it comes to racing. Having to memorise and apply a set of strict rules, avoid other boats in close proximity and sail in a certain direction to a mark can be daunting — *and* you still have to steer and trim efficiently, watch the breeze and not fall in when you gybe!

Crewing for an experienced sailor will give you the chance to observe someone else's sailing style at close quarters and pick up a few tips, as well as learn how to handle the jib and spinnaker (so you can advise your own crew later). You will also gain experience in how races are conducted — starting procedures, courses and so on — and learn how meeting situations and other rules work in real life, without running the risk of collisions in your own boat, or annoying other, more serious racers!

SAILING WITH OTHERS MEANS THAT THERE IS ALWAYS A READY PAIR OF HANDS TO HELP RIG, LAUNCH AND RETRIEVE.

CREWING FOR AN EXPERIENCED SAILOR IN A DOUBLE-HANDED CLASS IS A GOOD WAY TO FURTHER YOUR UNDERSTANDING OF THE SPORT AND EXPERIENCE RACING FIRST-HAND.

Working together

You may already know someone who is prepared to take you out on the water; alternatively, visit your local sailing club and talk to its members — someone is bound to take you up on your offer to crew. Skippers are often looking for crew — even inexperienced sailors — and as long as you do what you are told and are will-ing and able to learn, you will almost certainly be offered an opportunity to sail. Some skippers have a tendency to shout and can appear stressed during the heat of a race — but remember that it is seldom meant as a personal attack on you, but rather as a result of the level of concentration demanded by the skipper.

If you encounter someone who is unpleasant to sail with, or who criticises you and dents your confidence, don't be afraid to shop around until you find someone with whom you are compatible. You do not have to be harsh, rude and unpleasant to be a good sailor; in fact, the best skippers are usually those who remain calm and collected.

Dinghy cruising

If you do not have a competitive streak or are simply enjoying the experience of sailing too much to have it disturbed by start guns, tacking duels and protest hearings, then you can simply continue cruising. There will always be an opportunity to simply sail for pleasure on a sunny summer's day.

Some larger and more traditional dinghies will have room to stow provisions and spare clothes for day outings to local islands or bays you may pass en route. For classic inspiration on dinghy cruises, take a copy of Arthur Ransome's *Swallows and Amazons* series of books – great reads for the laid-back sailor!

Just remember, tell someone where you are going and when you expect to be back, plan your trip carefully and check the weather forecast so your relaxing day lying on a distant beach isn't followed by a four-hour beat home into 20 knots of wind! See also Safety first on page 13.

KEELBOATS CARRY LARGER GEAR AND CAN ACCOMMODATE BIGGER LOADS THAN A DINGHY, BUT THE SAILING PRINCIPLES ARE MUCH THE SAME FOR BOTH.

Keelboat sailing

The skills you learn dinghy sailing will translate easily onto sailing larger boats. The principles of making the boat sail are the same, and systems and set-ups are similar, although gear will obviously be bigger and the loads greater.

You may get the opportunity to sail on a sportsboat or a keelboat. Sportsboats are larger than dinghys but are still kept on a trailer or in a hardstanding area. They usually have a central keel with lead at its base for stability, which is lifted when the boat is taken out of the water, and are designed to be light and fast. They are usually between 5.5m and 8m long, and there is a wide range of designs and classes.

Keelboat is the collective name for any larger yacht that has a large, fixed, weighted keel protruding from the bottom of the hull, which gives them greater stability than a dinghy and helps them sail better to windward. To cope with the increased loads, most keelboats have winches to handle ropes, and large cleats to secure the sheets and halyards.

Utilizing your dinghy skills

Your grounding in dinghies will stand you in good stead for keelboats. You will be a more useful crew member than someone who has only sailed on keelboats and knows only one job, or part of it. To find a ride on a keelboat, contact your local sailing club and see if anyone needs crew.

Of course, keelboats and their smaller cousins, trailer sailers, which have a drop-down keel rather like a large, weighted centreboard and can be towed behind a car, are much more comfortable for cruising than your average dinghy! Most boats can be chartered with a skipper – very helpful for the less experienced – or, once you have a recognized boating qualification, you can charter bareboat and be your own skipper.

Of course, to take a boat overnight you need to know more than just how to sail – you need to master anchoring, know how yacht galleys (kitchens) and heads (toilets) work, how to read charts, coming alongside jetties and so on – so cruising with friends or a professional skipper is a good place to start.

Making contact

Most professional and national sailing clubs and associations are usually staffed by experienced sailors who have considerable insight into conditions and facilities in their particular region, and can offer sound advice as well as contact information to help you get in touch with a sailing club or school.

INTERNATIONAL SAILING FEDERATION (ISAF)

The ISAF is the controlling body of all forms of sailing throughout the world. Its role is to promote the sport in all its branches; oversee international yacht-racing rules; organize the Olympic regatta, and work closely with member authorities. Its website contains a comprehensive list of these at www.sailing.org/mna/mna.asp

- Ariadne House, Town Quay, Southampton, SO14 2AQ, UK
- Tel: + 44 (23) 806 35111
- Fax: + 44 (23) 806 35789
- Website: www.sailing.org

SAILING ASSOCIATIONS

ARGENTINA
- FEDERACION ARGENTINA DE YACHTING

- Venezuela 110 Piso 12 A, 1095, Buenos Aires, Argentina
- Tel: (11) 4342 6358
- Fax: (11) 4342 6358
- E-mail: fay@fay.org
- Website: www.fay.org

AUSTRALIA
- AUSTRALIAN YACHTING FEDERATION
- Locked Bag 806, Milsons Point, NSW 2061, Australia
- Tel: + 61 (2) 8424 7400
- Fax: + 61 (2) 9906 2366
- E-mail: training@yachting.org.au
- Website: www.yachting.org.au

BRAZIL
- FEDERACAO BRASILEIRA DE VELA E MOTOR
- Av. da Américas 500 Bloco 20 – Sala 310, Barra da Tijuca - RJ Rio de Janiero, 22640-100, Brasil
- Tel: + 55 (21) 3139 9200
- Fax: + 55 (21) 2495 4016
- E-mail: fbvm@fbvm.org.br
- Website: www.fbvm.org.br

CANADA
- CANADIAN YACHTING ASSOCIATION
- Portsmouth Olympic Harbour, 53 Yonge Street, Kingston, Ontario, K7M 6G4, Canada
- Tel: (613) 545 3044
- Fax: (613) 545 3045
- E-mail: sailcanada@sailing.ca
- Website: www.sailing.ca

FRANCE
- FEDERATION FRANCAISE DE VOILE
- 17 rue Henri Bocquillon 75015 Paris, France
- Tel: + 33 (1) 40 60 37 00
- Fax: + 33 (1) 40 60 37 37
- Website: www.ffvoile.org

GERMANY
- DEUTSCHER SEGLER-VERBAND
- Gruendgensstrasse 18 D-22309 Hamburg, Gernamy
- Tel: + 49 (40) 6320090
- Fax: + 49 (40) 6320092
- E-mail: regatta@dsv.org
- Website: www.dsv.org

HONG KONG
- HONG KONG SAILING FEDERATION
- Room 1009, Olympic House 1 Stadium Path, So Kon Po Causeway Bay, Hong Kong
- Tel: + (852) 2504 8159
- Fax: + (852) 2504 0681
- E-mail: hksf@sailing.org.hk
- Website: www.sailing.org.hk

IRELAND
- IRISH SAILING ASSOCIATION
- 3 Park Road, Dun Laoghaire, Co. Dublin, Ireland
- Tel: + 353 (1) 280 0239

- Fax: + 353 (1) 280 7558
- Email: info@sailing.ie
- Website: www.sailing.ie

ITALY

- **FEDERAZIONE ITALIANA VELA**
- Corte Lambruschini, Piazza
Borgo, Pila 40, Torre A — 16 Piano,
16129 Genova, Italy
- Tel: (010) 54 4541
- Fax: (010) 59 2864
- E-mail: federvela@federvela.it
- Website: www.federvela.it

JAPAN

- **JAPAN SAILING FEDERATION**
- Dr. Kishi Memorial Hall 1-1-1
Jinnan, Shibuya-ku, Tokyo 150-
8050, Japan
- Tel: (3) 3481 2357

- Fax: (3) 3481 0414
- Website: www.jsaf.or.jp

NEW ZEALAND

- **YACHTING NEW ZEALAND**
- PO Box 91 209, Victoria Street
West, Auckland 1142, New Zealand
- Tel: + 64 (9) 361 1471
- Fax: + 64 (9) 360 2246
- E-mail: mail@yachtingnz.org.nz
- Website: www.yachtingnz.org.nz

SOUTH AFRICA

- **SOUTH AFRICAN SAILING**
- PO Box 519, Paarden, 7420,
South Africa
- Tel: + 27 (21) 511 0929
- Fax: + 27 (21) 511 0965
- E-mail: mail@sailing.org.za
- Website: www.sailing.org.za

UNITED KINGDOM

- **ROYAL YACHTING ASSOCIATION**
- RYA House, Ensign Way, Hamble,
Hampshire, SO31 4YA, England
- Tel: + 44 (0)845 345 0400
- Fax: + 44 (0)845 345 0329
- E-mail: racing@rya.org.uk
- Website: www.rya.org.uk

USA

- **UNITED STATES SAILING
ASSOCIATION (US SAILING)**
- PO Box 1260, Portsmouth, RI
02871, USA
- Tel: (401) 683 0800
- Fax: (401) 683 0840
- E-mail: info@ussailing.org
- Website: www.ussailing.org

THE THRILL AND EXCITEMENT OF DINGHY SAILING HAS MADE IT ONE OF THE WORLD'S MOST POPULAR WATER SPORTS.

Glossary

Abeam Positioned in the centre of the boat.

Aft Positioned towards the back (also known as the stern) of the boat.

Astern Positioned behind the boat.

Backstays *See* stays.

Beam reaching Sailing off the wind, with the wind coming across the boat at a 90° angle.

Beam The widest part of the boat, usually in about the centre.

Bearing away The action of steering the boat's bow away from the direction of the wind. Also known as 'coming down'.

Beating Sailing upwind, using the action of tacking. *See also* tacking.

Boom vang The control rope that runs from the underside of the boom down to the lower part of the mast. The boom vang is used to keep the boom down and under control.

Boom The horizontal pole, attached to the mast at right angles, to which the bottom edge of the mainsail is attached.

Bow Front end of the boat. Also called the 'stem'.

Brace *See* guy.

Broad reaching Broad reaching is sailing off the wind with the wind coming from an angle of more than 90° to the beam.

Clew The aft corner of a sail.

Close reaching Sailing slightly off the wind with the sails slightly eased. Also called 'tight reaching'.

Close-hauled *See* upwind.

Cockpit The area indented into the deck where the crew sit and from which they sail the boat.

Coming down *See* bearing away.

Coming up *See* luffing up.

Cunningham The control rope that runs from the tack of the mainsail down to the deck or in the cockpit; used to adjust the tension of the luff of the sail.

Deck The flat area that covers the top surface of the boat.

Downwind Sailing in any direction, with the wind coming from behind the boat. Objects or destinations can also be referred to as 'downwind' of your current position if your boat is positioned between the object/destination and the direction from which the wind is blowing. Downwind is also known as 'sailing off the wind'.

Easing *See* trimming.

Flat off *See* running.

Foot The bottom of a sail.

Foresail *See* jib.

Forestay *See* stays.

Forward Towards the front (or bow) of the boat. Usually pronounced *for'ard*.

Gennaker An asymmetrical downwind sail, usually flown with one corner fixed to a bowsprit or prod sticking out of the front of the boat.

Genoa *See* jib.

Gooseneck A flexible fitting connecting the mast and boom, which allows the boom to swing through an angle of up to 180°, from side to side.

Gunwales The top edges of the boat, at the upper edge of the topsides. Pronounced *gunnels*.

Guy The sheet running from the fixed corner of the spinnaker and back to the cockpit. This is used to adjust the fore and aft position of the spinnaker pole. Also known as the 'brace'.

Gybing Changing direction when sailing downwind, so that the stern passes through the eye of the wind.

Halyards The lines used to haul sails up into position and hold them there.

Hard-on *See* upwind.

Head The top corner of a sail.

Headsail *See* jib.

Hull The solid part of the boat that sits in the water.

Jib Smaller than the mainsail, flown in front of the mast. Also known as 'headsail', 'foresail' or 'genoa'.

Kicker *See* boom vang.

Leach The trailing edge of a sail.

Leeward The direction away from which the wind is blowing. Pronounced *loo-ard*.

Luff The leading edge of a sail

Luffing up The action of steering the boat's bow up into or towards the direction of the wind to bring the boat onto an upwind course, or beyond it. Also known as 'coming up'.

Mainsail The largest sail, flown aft of the mast.

Mast The vertical wooden, metal or composite pole (that protrudes from the middle of the boat) from which the sails are flown.

Off the wind *See* downwind.

On the wind *See* upwind.

Outhaul The control rope that runs between the clew of the mainsail and the aft end of the boom; used to adjust the foot of the sail.

Point of sail The angle to the wind at which a boat is sailing.

Port The nautical term for 'left'. The port side of the boat is the left-hand side of the boat when you are facing forward.

Reaching Sailing off the wind at an angle of between 45°–175° to the wind direction.

Rigging The various items of equipment attached to the boat's hull and decks.

Running rigging The ropes and other adjustable fittings on the boat.

Running Sailing an angle of 180° to the wind direction. Also known as 'sailing flat off'.

Sheeting *See* trimming.

Sheets The lines used to control the sails. These are specified according to the sails to which they are attached, e.g mainsheet, jib sheet, spinnaker sheet.

Shrouds *See* stays.

Sidestays *See* stays.

Spars The mast and boom.

Spinnaker A symmetrical, curved downwind sail, flown off its own boom, forward of the mast.

Standing rigging The stays that hold up the mast.

Starboard The nautical term for 'right'; used in the same way as 'port'.

Stays The stays are the individual rigging wires that hold the mast upright and in the right position. These wire ropes usually lead down to the bow (the forestay) and to the sides of the boat, parallel with the mast (sidestays or shrouds). Sometimes, there is also a stay (or stays) leading to the stern of the boat (backstays).

Stem *See* bow.

Stern The back end of the boat.

Tack The forward corner of a sail.

Tacking Changing direction when sailing upwind, so that the bow of the boat passes through the eye of the wind.

Tight reaching Sailing slightly off the wind with the sails slightly eased. Also called 'close reaching'.

Topsides The part of the hull above the water.

Transom The flat, vertical area at the stern of the boat, to which the rudder is attached.

Trimming Pulling the ropes attached to the sails to change their shape and harness the wind. Pulling them in is called 'sheeting' or 'trimming'. The opposite of 'trimming' is easing, when the sheets are let out. Sails are said to be correctly trimmed when they are adjusted for maximum efficiency and air flow.

Upwind Sailing as close to the wind direction as possible. Also known as 'sailing hard on', 'sailing on the wind', 'sailing close-hauled' (because all the sails are pulled right in), 'sailing to windward' or 'beating'. This term is also used to refer generally to objects, destinations, etc. that are 'to windward' of your current position (they are, in other words, between you and the direction from which the wind is blowing).

Vang *See* boom vang.

Wharf Also generally known as a 'jetty' or 'dock'.

White horses Foaming crests on waves that are about to break. Caused by winds stronger than Force 3.

Windward The direction from which the wind is blowing. The windward side of the boat is the side closest to the way the wind is blowing. Also known as the 'weather side'.

Index

Photographic Credits

All photographs by Michael Ng/New Holland Image Library, with the exception of the following: **Nick Aldridge/NHIL:** front flap, pp 79 (except for Fig. B), 80–81; **Christel Clear:** pp 2, 73, 8 (bottom), 9, 10, 11 (right), 12, 15, 21 (left), 23, 24 (right), 26 (left), 27 (left and right), 28 (top), 34 (bottom), 35, 42 (top), 43, 54 (bottom), 56, 58 (far right), 71, 77 (left), 85, 86 (top and bottom), 90 (top and bottom), 93; **John Nash:** pp 24 (left), 31 (bottom), 77 (right); **Ocean Images:** pp 4–5, 6, 8 (top), 11 (left), 13, 14 (top), 22 (top), 25, 29, 34 (top), 55, 70 (top), 74, 76, 84 (top), 87, 88, 91; **PPL:** cover, pp 22 (bottom), 48, 62, 69; **Alain Proust/Struik Image Library:** p 89; **David Rogers/NHIL:** p 79 (Fig. B); **SSM/Joan Carter:** p 75.